Dear Ashley

Dear Ashley

*A Father's Reflections
and Letters to
His Daughter on Life,
Love and Hope*

DON BLACKWELL

IMBUE PUBLISHING
an Imprint of Morgan James Publishing
NEW YORK

Dear Ashley

A Father's Reflections and Letters to His Daughter on Life, Love and Hope

Disclaimer: The Publisher and the Author make no representations or warranties with respect to the accuracy or completeness of the contents of this work and specifically disclaim all warranties, including without limitation warranties of fitness for a particular purpose. No warranty may be created or extended by sales or promotional materials. The advice and strategies contained herein may not be suitable for every situation. This work is sold with the understanding that the Publisher is not engaged in rendering legal, accounting, or other professional services. If professional assistance is required, the services of a competent professional person should be sought. Neither the Publisher nor the Author shall be liable for damages arising herefrom. The fact that an organization or website is referred to in this work as a citation and/or a potential source of further information does not mean that the Author or the Publisher endorses the information the organization or website may provide or recommendations it may make. Further, readers should be aware that internet websites listed in this work may have changed or disappeared between when this work was written and when it is read.

ISBN 978-1-61448-329-8 paperback
ISBN 978-1-61448-330-4 eBook
Library of Congress Control Number:

Imbue Publishing
an Imprint of Morgan James Publishing
The Entrepreneurial Publisher
5 Penn Plaza, 23rd Floor,
New York City, New York 10001
(212) 655-5470 office • (516) 908-4496 fax
www.MorganJamesPublishing.com

Cover Design by:
Rachel Lopez
www.r2cdesign.com

Interior Design by:
Bonnie Bushman
bonnie@caboodlegraphics.com

In an effort to support local communities, raise awareness and funds, Morgan James Publishing donates a percentage of all book sales for the life of each book to Habitat for Humanity Peninsula and Greater Williamsburg.

Get involved today, visit
www.MorganJamesBuilds.com.

DEDICATION

To my daughter, Ashley:
I would have given anything, including my very life, to have
spared you from the unimaginable suffering and heartache
that ultimately led me to the reflections and revelations that
fill the following pages. I only hope that the life lessons I've
learned through your pain and what, perhaps unbeknownst
to you, became our mutual struggle for understanding and
emotional survival, will enable another precious young
woman and her family to find hope and shed one less tear in
their collective journey towards a full recovery.
You are my inspiration.
Dad

And to Cyndy, my wife and Ashley's mom,
whose selfless and tireless devotion to our daughter during
her illness served as a daily reminder to Ashley that she is
loved unconditionally, and that she is worthy of love.

TABLE OF CONTENTS

The Healing

FOREWORD

By Michael E. Berrett, PhD

This book, *Dear Ashley… A Father's Reflections and Letters to His Daughter on Life, Love, and Hope*, is a beautiful, refreshing, and inspiring message. It can be a powerful tool in the work of recovery from the pain and suffering of eating disorder illnesses, for the patient, their families, and professionals. However, it is also a lesson in high-quality, close proximity, and deeply engaged parenting. The lessons taught can be applied well beyond the suffering of eating disorders, and into any loving relationship towards living a life with a positive attitude, courage, integrity, and love.

It is a privilege to write this Foreword.

I have been treating those suffering with eating disorders for more than 28 years. It has been my honor to be in the trenches with courageous clients and their families, doing battle with these deadly illnesses. Gratefully, I have also learned that full recovery is possible, and that there is great reason to have much hope in this worthy cause.

x | *Dear Ashley*

I met Don after a speaking engagement in South Florida. I was at the podium, and Don was in the audience. After my speech, Don was kind and gracious enough to approach me and let me know that his daughter suffered with anorexia. He said he was grateful that I had been willing in my presentation to discuss my experience in also having a beautiful and wonderful daughter in the grasp of an eating disorder. We made a connection. We both knew something of the feelings of guilt, inadequacy, fear, and helplessness as fathers of one so suffering.

My moments of vulnerability and sharing in that community presentation apparently touched Don in some way. Now, the tables have been turned. In reading his beautiful book, Don is at the podium, and I have found myself in the audience as a learner. I have been taught well and feel deeply inspired by his stories and his words of wisdom. His book has touched me, lifted me, and given me an example of how to live as a parent of one who is suffering from an eating disorder.

In the eating disorder treatment field, various theories about the causes, solutions and treatments of these illnesses have cycled in and out of prominence. Gratefully, the days of misplaced and hurtful blame on parents and families for these complex illnesses are mainly in the past. The pendulum has swung back, and now parents are again feeling empowered to feed and parent their children. In this backswing, however, we may have created a climate where an open discussion on parenting is difficult to have without offending some professionals or parents.

Don's book is a model and example of what can be and needs to be done. It is a bridge between the two ends of a spectrum, with a powerful message that while parents are not responsible for the development of their child's eating disorder illness, parents do have the responsibility, and the privilege, to engage in a loving relationship which does not include any measure of "holding back". He teaches that the true power in parenting comes not from hiding real human weakness and various feelings of inadequacy, but by telling the truth about them, and then moving beyond them with the power of love and influence. Don is a pioneer and an example to us all in the mastery of "positive self-disclosure," where humility, openness, and vulnerability lift and empower.

The book teaches that lives can be touched through three important steps: 1) observation of unfolding stories, 2) honest self-reflection and application, and 3) sharing what we have learned with those whom we love and care about.

Don takes readers through this three-step process, as he writes about many key principles of character which empower recovery including faith, honesty, courage, and perseverance. He teaches us about living life fully, learning to love, and the processes of surrender, recovery, and healing. He teaches us what he has learned through observation and self-honesty, and then he teaches us what he has taught his daughter Ashley, through personal, tender and heartfelt letters.

Don also gives us a glimpse of the important role that faith in God has had in his life and in the lives of his family. Without any attempt to sell a particular brand of religious faith or spirituality, he gracefully reminds us all that spirituality is at the core of recovery, and that finding again faith in self, family, professionals, the future, recovery, and God can begin to heal the ravages of an eating disorder.

I highly recommend this book, which comes from a brilliant writer, tender-hearted father, and a man of faith and integrity. It will tug at your heart strings and inspire deep self-reflection. It will invite you to stand up and reach a little higher in receiving and giving love and tenderness beyond the obstacles of fear or self-doubt.

Parents, families, patients, professionals, and individuals in general will be greatly rewarded and well-taught by jumping into this easy-to-read and difficult-to-forget-book, which has a spirit of honesty, goodness, and illumination. It is a testament not only that recovery is possible, but that tender parental love is also possible, enduring, and of great worth.

I am happy to know that Don's wonderful daughter Ashley is enjoying her life in a place of recovery. I am likewise grateful to report that my wondrous daughter, who suffered with bulimia, has also traveled the difficult pathway to recovery.

I will forever be grateful to Don for teaching me more about how awareness, self-honesty, vulnerability, and courage to express love can prevail above self-protection and fear.

Sincerely,

Michael

Michael E. Berrett, PhD
Psychologist, CEO, Co-founder, Center for Change
Co-author, APA Book, *Spiritual Approaches in the Treatment of Women with Eating Disorders*

PREFACE

From the time I was able to think independently until well into adulthood, I always recoiled whenever someone greeted news of a traumatic life event (*e.g.*, a critical illness, death, a marital break-up, etc.) by trotting out their belief that "everything happens for a reason." Like most clichés, its use seemed intellectually and emotionally lazy. Moreover, because it was seldom accompanied by any attempt to articulate what those reasons might be, the adage offered little consolation or encouragement, particularly to those who found themselves in the grip of the underlying trauma. To the contrary, if anything, the sentiment seemed dismissive, if not heartless. Most importantly, in my mind, embracing that belief meant relegating us to little more than automatons dangling helplessly on the ends of the strings of a Divine Puppeteer or the whims of fate—concepts that simply did not coincide with my evolving belief system.

I now realize, however, largely as a result of a life-threatening illness involving my daughter, that what the proponents of that belief more precisely mean to convey is that, while events and situations may seem xiv | *Dear Ashley*

(and often are) inexplicably tragic and traumatic as they are unfolding, they can also serve as critical points of reflection and opportunities for growth. I also realize that if we are willing to take a step back from the heartbreak of the moment and reflect on the matters of the heart that surround those events, they can lead to a deeper understanding of ourselves, of those we love and of the human condition.

In the pages that follow, I attempt to capture that reality, using illustrations drawn from my own life and the people (real and fictional) who have been an integral part of it. At first blush, some of those people and characters will seem to the reader to be unlikely sources of support for my thesis, while others will be far more obvious.

Each chapter is built around one of those people, and though loosely woven into a whole, is intended to serve as an independent source of reflection for the reader. To further that objective, each chapter includes a letter that I wrote to my daughter—some of which were sent to her in the course of her treatment, others in the course of my writing this book. In addition, at the end of the book is an Appendix, which contains a collection of publicly available, supplemental source materials that the reader can access at his or her leisure as additional points of reflection on the themes discussed in each of the chapters. In some instances, those source materials (and the chapters themselves) include Biblical references, which highlight the timelessness of the principle explored in the chapter. To those of faith, the Biblical references are intended to add yet another layer of reflection to the reading experience. To those questioning their faith or of a different faith, as well as those of no religious faith, they are offered for consideration, the acceptance or non-acceptance of which will not detract from the book's message or import.

One final caveat: I am not a medical doctor, nor am I a psychologist. I am a 53-year-old South Florida attorney, who, at various times, has been a number of other things—a dad, a husband, a brother, a son, a writer, a poet, a youth league baseball coach, a teacher, a friend, a college disc jockey, a boss, a charity event organizer, a teammate, the new kid in town, a problem-solver, a shoulder to cry on, a peace-seeker and maker, and a dreamer—to name just a few. This book and the words in it come straight from my heart. They are the by-product of a lifetime of searching, of questioning and, more recently, of listening. In sharing them, my intent is not to provide answers or a "how-to" guide of some kind, but rather to provoke thought, to stimulate action, and ultimately to be a source of inspiration, healing and hope.

ACKNOWLEDGEMENTS

Although this book was very much a labor of love, it simply would not have been possible to complete it without the patience, candor, guidance, and editorial skill of Michele Rothkopf to whom I am eternally grateful. I also owe a considerable debt of gratitude to Stephanie Martinez, a colleague and friend who endured countless hours of me curled up on the floor in a corner of her office, sharing and offering her feedback on my latest inspiration or ideas for a new chapter and who, on more than one occasion, "talked me down off the ledge" when writer's block set in or, worse yet, I thought of abandoning the project entirely. Her and Michele's steadfast belief in this book and insistence that I finish it likely are the reason you are reading these words today. In addition, I want to thank all those who supported me throughout this process, including Henry Rojas, Dr. Jennifer Nardozzi, Dr. Richard MacKenzie, Robert Torricella and Bruce Stanley—to name just a few. Their belief in me, in Ashley and in the importance of this book and its message factored prominently in my dedication and determination to see it through to completion, even though it often meant reliving experiences that challenged me to the core. Finally, I want to thank all those who, either through the examples of their lives or their writings or both have helped me to be the man and the dad I am today.

A GRADUATION NOTE

Gulliver Commencement
The Next Day, Wednesday, May 31, 2006
7:00 am

Dear Ashley,

I wish I could begin to capture in words the hundreds of thoughts, memories, and emotions that flooded into my mind and my heart as you crossed the stage of the Bank United Center last night to receive your high school diploma—that I could adequately communicate the tremendous sense of pride I feel (and have felt) over the past 18 years, as I have watched you grow and develop into the remarkable young woman you are today and accomplish things that are almost incomprehensible for someone so young. Where would I begin... Should I start with your unparalleled accomplishments in the classroom: your achievement of the distinction of being a National Merit Scholarship Finalist; your recognition as a Gold Key recipient in this year's Scholastic Writing Competition; your selection to be a Presidential Scholar at the

University of Southern California; the myriad of glowing comments you have received from your professors at Gulliver over the years, recognizing, among other things, your diligence, your creativity, your enthusiasm and your ever-present quest for excellence, a quest that ultimately led some of the finest Universities in the country to extend an invitation for you to join their academic communities? That certainly would seem to be a logical starting point, given that it is graduation day.

But, perhaps I should start, instead, with your accomplishments in the performing arts: the fact that you were one of only a handful of high school students in the entire State of Florida to have earned a coveted spot on the All-State Reading Choir in 3 of your 4 years at Gulliver and the only freshman in Gulliver history to have been so honored; the joy and goodwill that you and your friends at the Miami Children's Chorus brought with you to thousands of appreciative concertgoers in South Florida and in Europe over the years; your and the Gulliver Choir's countless "Superior" ratings by panels of chorale experts around the State of Florida, which, among other things, earned you the privilege of performing at Carnegie Hall—an experience most can only dream about— and, ultimately, the most coveted individual awards Gulliver has to offer a member of its vocal ensembles; the fact that, in two auditions, you earned roles in two motion pictures, "The Boynton Beach Club" and "My Sexiest Year"—and, later, the adulation of not one, but two, prominent Hollywood directors; and your indispensable role in the founding and success of Rearview Mirror Productions. Because many of these accomplishments occurred beyond school walls, a number of them went unnoticed by friends, teachers and administrators at Gulliver, but all of them made a profound impact on those whose lives you've touched with your smile, your creativity, and your love for music and acting, including mine.

As magnificent as all of those achievements are, however (and make no mistake about it, they are extraordinary), they are, in my mind, only a small part of what makes you exceptional—"you" are what makes you exceptional… your spirit, your character, your compassion, your love and concern for others, your insight, your creativity, your independence, your sensitivity to others' needs and feelings, your knowledge of right and wrong, your desire to do what's right, your loyalty, your unwavering commitment to people and to tasks, your integrity, your dreams and ambitions, your motivation and self-discipline, and your work ethic. These are the things that make you unique and they are the gifts that will allow you to achieve your goals. In case you've missed it along the way (or worse yet, in case there were times when I neglected to tell you) there has never been a moment in the last eighteen years that I haven't been proud of you or thanked God for your presence in my life—last night was no exception. Please don't take this the wrong way, but I can't wait for you to leave home, not because I am anxious to see you go (actually a piece of my heart will leave with you), but because I am anxious for the rest of the world to more fully experience the remarkable gift that is you.

Thanks for allowing me to be part of the journey.

With All My Love,
Dad

And then, less than three months later, for reasons that science and medicine still can't explain, my daughter—the brightest, most creative, most passionate person I have ever known—stopped eating.

INTRODUCTION

A few years ago, while sitting in a local church listening to the Old Testament story of Moses and the burning bush (Exodus 2:23–3:20), it occurred to me that maybe God is over the whole burning bush thing. Oh sure, there undoubtedly still are life situations where those involved experience a "burning bush moment." However, my sense is that, more often than not, God chooses to be much more subtle when it comes to showing His face to us and that we, in turn, are called upon to be much more sensitive to and perceptive of His presence in the world and His efforts to provide guidance to us on our life journeys. As I started to look at my life through the prism of that possibility, I began to see seemingly ordinary people and events in my and others' everyday lives in an entirely different and extraordinary way.

A CASE IN POINT: THE BABY

Our now 24-year old daughter, Ashley, who, for the better part of five years fought what quite literally became a life-and-death battle with anorexia nervosa, has never been very fond of children, particularly infants. I'm not entirely sure where or why her aversion first began, but it's real. In fact, if you were to believe what she's had to say on the subject over the years, her aversion has, at times, bordered on open hostility. So you can imagine my surprise, when, in the days leading up to my church pew revelation, I received a call from her gushing about a brief experience she had earlier that day with a baby, whom a friend had asked her to hold during family visitation at the treatment facility where both of them were residents at the time. She too was surprised when the baby took to her almost immediately. He had smiled from ear to ear while she was holding him, reached out his arms to her lovingly and enthusiastically, and when the time came for him to be returned to his mother, he insisted on hugging her not once, but twice.

The smile in her voice while recounting the day's events was evident even over the telephone, a brief but no less welcomed change in a spirit that, in the preceding months, had been repeatedly ravaged to the point of despair by an insidious and extremely complex disease that often left our daughter, a young woman once steeped in faith, questioning the very existence of God, if not openly suggesting that He had abandoned her entirely.

Still, I didn't think too much of it at the time—reluctant to place too much importance on what seemed like a relatively commonplace event in the midst of the gathering storm that had characterized her disease—that is until several days later in that church pew, when, looking through my new-found prism, I saw her experience with the baby in a completely different light. I rushed home from church and quickly sent my daughter the following note:

Dear Ashley:

> *I was thinking about that baby you told me about last week, the one who hugged you so lovingly and enthusiastically, and then did it again—just in case you missed it the first time! Truth is,*

Ash, I think both of us may have missed it the first time, but it is very clear to me now: What if it was no accident that the baby found his way into your unsuspecting arms? What if that adorable little child was the manifestation of the God who created and is committed to protecting you? What if it was His way of telling you: "I am here for you, Ashley, I love you, and I will never abandon you?"

With All My Love,
Dad

And so began my journey…

The Hurt

CHAPTER 1

On Loneliness and Intimacy

("Dealing with it just like all the other kids"—or not)

I've always envied people who are able not only to remember the names of many of their elementary, middle and high school classmates, but who still count some of them among their closest friends. I have very few memories of my childhood and early adolescence, let alone of those outside my immediate family who shared those periods of my life with me—inside or outside the classroom. I suppose part of that is a by-product of having grown up in a home with a father whose job kept the family constantly on the move from one city to the next. Knowing that another move to a distant city was always just around the corner probably didn't have a significant impact on me in the early years, but, over time, it made it increasingly difficult to develop or even want to consider developing the kinds of close friendships that I suspect often arise between those who, year after year, are fortunate to share the experiences of growing up in a common community.

I also don't remember my mom and dad socializing much with other families who had children our age or taking other affirmative steps to help facilitate our getting acclimated to our new surroundings and making new friends. To the contrary, my recollection is that my brother, sister and I were largely on our own where relationship-making and building was concerned, and if I'm to be honest, we weren't afforded much in the way of a model as to how to make that happen or what a healthy relationship between a man and a woman, a man and a man, a woman and a woman, brothers and sisters or a parent and a child was supposed to look like. I did, however, have a very clear picture as to what healthy relationships did not look like. Simply put, there was a lot of loneliness and a lack of intimacy in my childhood home.

Initially, I tried to fill that void with activities that I knew would keep me busy and out of the house for extended periods of time and which weren't dependent on others' availability—sports like golf and bowling. Sometimes, I would spend hours hitting plastic golf balls from one sprinkler head to the next in our front yard or take a "shag bag" out to an adjacent easement, where I would pound balls between telephone poles that Florida Power & Light had conveniently placed 150 yards apart until it was too dark to find them in the seldom mown grass. As I grew older, a nearby driving range and practice facility that was lit in the evenings became my second home—my refuge. In fact, that was the place I spent what was to have been the night of my high school senior prom—a long story for another time!

Inevitably, of course, I had to come home, and when I did, I spent much of my time in my room alone, writing poetry and letters and listening to music. In fact, I spent so much time by myself that it probably appeared to others that I actually preferred to be alone, and yet the truth was that I longed for nothing more than real companionship, someone to care about and who cared about me.

Interestingly, I found myself gravitating towards female friends. For some reason, I felt a closer connection to them. They shared the way I thought and felt about things much more than my few guy friends did. They tended to be more sensitive, more introspective, more in touch with matters of the heart, and considerably less superficial. They, in turn, viewed me as different from most guys, someone they could confide in when a problem arose, a problem-solver, a friend who, in their mind, was non-threatening, so non-threatening, in fact that, more than once, I ended up being the proverbial "third wheel" on dates they had with some of my best guy friends. We were one big happy teenage family—or so they thought. Unfortunately, I often grew to want more out of those relationships, but on those few occasions when I mustered the courage to reach out and suggest that, my overtures were mostly ignored, ostensibly so as not to "ruin a perfectly good friendship."

I let it ride because I too wasn't willing to make a trade between no relationships at all and the relationships I truly wanted. The last thing I wanted was to feel even more abandoned than I already did. Nothing was worth that—or so I thought. Unbeknownst to me, however, each time it happened, I was hearing and internalizing a much different message than the messengers likely ever knowingly intended to send. It was the same message that always seemed to reverberate off the walls in my childhood home: "Don, maybe if you were just a little different, a little better, a little more productive, a little more compliant, a little more perfect, a little more or less something, you'd get the love you want and need."

The effect of that message also was always the same—I tried a little harder to be a little "better" and, at the same time, grew incrementally more insecure, more uncertain about whether I was doing enough, and more importantly, whether what I had to give would ever be good enough. And then I had children of my own, and I swore to myself that things would be different for them, that I would do everything I could to let them know how very much they were loved at home. I wanted to shield them from the incomparable hurt that comes from feeling alone and unloved, as if there were something about them that somehow made them unlovable.

Unfortunately, time and circumstances have shown me that only so much of being able to keep that promise was within my control. The rest is left to the world at large, a world that, regrettably, is growing increasingly less intimate and more impersonal by the minute, particularly where those most in need of true intimacy are concerned— our young people. What once was a neighbor's afterschool knock on the door asking if my brother, sister or I could come out and play has long since been replaced by text messages, instant messaging, "tweeting" and endless hours on social networking sites. In fact, these forms of communication have fundamentally altered the way all of us interact with each other and have become not only the principal, but the preferred means by which children, adolescents and young adults communicate with each other. They also are a common method of communicating for adults, for business people, for spouses, for friends, for next door neighbors and even, in too many instances, for parents and their children.

Along the way, words, indeed entire sentences, have been replaced by acronyms, thoughts and feelings are often reduced to what can fit in 140 characters or less, and smiley faces and other symbols have been substituted, in the name of expediency, perhaps even laziness, for the radiant in-person smile and other facial expressions of a friend or lover. Cell phones, PDAs and laptops are our new lifeline to the outside world, a world that we don't even have to leave the security of our bedrooms to explore. It's all right there at our fingertips, a few key strokes away—everything, that is, except true friendship and physical companionship, the most fundamental needs of the human heart.

It is an irrefutable reality that the Creator has known from the beginning of time: "It is not good for man to be alone." Genesis 2:18. Indeed, I believe that, in His infinite wisdom, God has been erecting living, breathing neon signs around us ever since in the hope that we would come to that same realization and react to it accordingly. We fail to do so at considerable peril to ourselves and to those we profess to love, because if I have learned anything from listening to my heart over the past several years, as well as the wailings of hearts trapped in bodies ravaged by eating disorders and other addictions in hospitals and treatment centers around the country, it is that nothing paralyzes the soul, mind and body more profoundly or more completely than loneliness. If I'm right, then stepping away from the multiple keyboards that exist in all of our lives and allowing ourselves to be fully present in the lives of others just could make all the difference in the world.

Dear Ashley,

I received the following letter when I was 34 years old. While I'd like to think it was not the first time my dad was proud of me, I'm fairly certain it was the first time he ever used words to tell me he was. I framed it:

May 20, 1992

Dear Don,

I have almost recovered from your sterling "World Series Victory" of Saturday last. It was as the shouts of your exuberant team declared to the heavens—"AWESOME!"

The thing I need to comment on is how impressed I was with the conduct of the head coach. I couldn't help but think how lucky that collection of "All-Stars" was to have a man like you directing them.

No matter the circumstances, your every word to that team and its individual players was one of encouragement. In the darkest moments (10 runs down, for instance), you were constantly assuring one and all that collectively they had the ability not to just fight back, but to win.

Wherever the circumstances dictated despair, you instilled belief. What a marvelous gift that is—the absolute keystone in successful adult-child communication (if I sound jealous, it's because I am). The real uniqueness of your style, however, stems from your ability to convey your very special talent in such an enthusiastic, patiently positive manner. And miraculously, you manage to convey it to groups and individuals, as the situation dictates, with equal fervor and with exquisite timeliness.

The result speaks for itself. How sweet Saturday's victory was. I know much sweeter victories lie ahead.

As special as watching the comeback was for your mother and I, I am compelled to say, one more time, how very proud I was of your performance and how fortunate the youngsters are who came under your influence today, as well as those who will be touched by it in the years ahead.

On their behalf, I thank you for so generously sharing your time, your talent, your life and your love.

Love, Dad

In fact, that letter still hangs in my office to this day. It is one of the many reasons I can't possibly tell you and your brother often enough how very proud I am of you.

With All My Love,
Dad

CHAPTER 2

Daddy's Little Girl

(Walking unsuspectingly in our father's footsteps)

Well into our daughter's illness, which presented in an unusually acute and aggressive manner, a lifelong friend of mine who specializes in adolescent psychiatry cautioned me not to devote too much time and emotional energy searching for the "why" of her disease. She told me that I likely never would find a satisfactory answer to that question, since even those who have devoted their entire professional lives to the search have not yet reached a consensus on the myriad of genetic, physiological, sociological and emotional factors that almost certainly play some role in the disease process.

She also warned me against getting drawn into the "family blame game" that some in the eating disorder ("ED") treatment world are prone to play. The rules of the game are fairly simple. In it, the ED sufferer's parents and siblings, as well as the family unit as a whole, are painstakingly dissected, either in the parents' presence or in individual or group therapy sessions, as part of an equally misguided, real-life scavenger hunt for the root causes of the sufferer's disease, presumably so that once identified, those causes can be "repaired," or better yet, permanently removed.

Instead, my friend encouraged me to stay focused on the practical, but very critical, tasks at hand (*i.e.*, ensuring that Ashley was medically stable and that she returned to a life-sustaining weight with competent medical supervision) so that all of us could have the physical and emotional stamina required for the difficult journey to recovery that lay ahead. Try as I might, however, I found it nearly impossible not to repeatedly scour the landscape of my then 20-year relationship with my daughter in search of a clue that might explain how all of us arrived on the doorstep of her small L.A. apartment several years ago.

Turns out, of course, my friend was right. Despite more sleepless nights than I care to think about, I have yet to find a way to make the pieces of this very complex puzzle fit together neatly, if at all. However, the exercise of reflecting on my own personal journey with my daughter hasn't been for naught. Along the way, I remembered: the day I first learned that we would be welcoming a new member into our family, the early signs that it would be a difficult pregnancy, disturbing talk of possible complications, doctors' recommendations that we consider terminating the pregnancy due to the risk that those complications could result in deformities, including a loss of limbs as she developed, our agonizing over and then rejecting that advice, confident that God's will would be done, and the months of bed-rest that followed.

I also vividly remembered being awakened VERY EARLY on a January morning, 6 weeks prior to her scheduled arrival date, with the news that Ashley apparently had decided not to wait (like her dad, patience has never been one of her strong suits!), watching anxiously as the fetal heart monitor fluctuated wildly for no apparent reason, and then being hurriedly escorted into a very tense operating room where doctors performed an emergency C-section and then unwrapped what seemed like several feet of umbilical cord from around our newborn daughter's neck, while she struggled to catch her breath and I held my own. I remembered how incredibly small and fragile she seemed at that indescribably beautiful moment, my taking a quick Reagan-esque inventory of her limbs (just to be sure the doctors' fears had not materialized—"trust but verify"!), and the nurses whisking all 4 pounds of her off to the neo-natal intensive care unit. I remembered the unsightly plexi-glass incubator where she would spend the first 10 days of her life and the vision of her laying there, helpless, with tubes and monitors protruding from every square inch of her body. I remembered leaving the hospital without her and being scared to death that she might never come home.

I remembered the day she left the hospital and the overwhelming sense of relief and gratitude I felt simply knowing she was alive. I remembered the piercing sound and intensity of her screams at bath time, which she hated as a baby. I remembered fearing that the large tumor on her shoulder that appeared overnight just before her second birthday was malignant, only to learn days later from the surgeon who surgically removed it that it was benign. I remembered her not wanting to be held or coddled and yet how anxious she became whenever she was pried away from her mom.

I remembered her being unusually creative and bright from an early age, not to mention stubborn as the proverbial mule! I remembered a mind that seemingly never stopped working and a heart filled with boundless compassion for others and for animals, especially horses and dogs. I remembered the hours she spent playing dress-up and Pet Shop with a neighborhood friend, a voracious appetite for reading, and quiet times with mom and dad at day's end sharing bedtime stories and saying prayers.

I remembered what, on reflection, were too many beautiful spring afternoons spent at little league baseball parks, particularly to a daughter likely longing for some alone time with a dad who already spent too much time at work. I remembered getting a call en route back from an out-of-town trip and racing to a local emergency room to find her strapped to a hospital bed with a badly fractured hip from a horseback riding accident that just as easily could have fractured her neck or claimed her life. I remembered that summer spent in a body cast and, less than 6 months later, watching her get back on that horse, whom she loved deeply, and riding off into the pasture as if nothing had happened—a profound display of courage and a touching moment of forgiveness and reconciliation between two old friends. I remembered penguins nipping at her shoelaces during a father/daughter trip to Sea World, our traveling to Charlotte to see Celine Dion in concert, time spent watching local productions of Broadway plays, accompanying her to auditions, and a very special ski trip to Smuggler's Notch—and I remembered thinking there should have been more of those times.

I remembered how much I loved to hear her sing and watch her act, and listening with pride to stories brought back from Europe where she and the other members of the Miami Children's Chorus entertained appreciative audiences in each of their native tongues. I remembered summer vacations at Ocean Isle Beach, hours spent bobbing in the surf, afternoons spent carefully constructing sand castles, trips to (and down) the neighborhood water slide, outings to every mini-golf course and ice cream parlor within 20 miles of "The Wright House," long walks to the pier and hush puppies with honey butter. I also remembered wishing I had taken more vacations and spent fewer holidays away from home.

I remembered our breakfast talks at Starbuck's on the way to my dropping her off at school and her sharing her writings with me— poems, short stories, plays, even the beginnings of a remarkably insightful novel—a satirical look at teenage life and love. I remembered a darkness, a solitariness and an intensity to her writings that caused me concern, and I wondered, looking back, whether they were intended, on some level, to convey the desperation that likely already was forming or may well have taken root in her soul. I remembered not wanting to pry, feeling a need to respect her privacy and never being quite certain where the proper boundary lines were between those feelings and my genuine concern for her emotional well-being.

I remembered wishing that she had been able to spend more time with her five cousins so that she would have a sense of extended family that I never knew and could benefit from the friendship and support of those relationships for a lifetime. I remembered, on many occasions, hoping that she and her brother would become closer friends, and in the process, be able to share and learn from each other's experiences and know that, if all else failed, one of their best friends was just down the hall. At the same time, I remembered never being quite sure what, if anything, I could do to facilitate the development of that bond, since, again, I had no experience to draw on in that critical area.

More importantly, I remembered that somewhere along the way, I formulated the belief, on a conscious or subconscious level, that Ashley didn't require my full attention— that she not only had the capacity, but the desire, to be independent. I, of all people, should have known better. I should have seen my own childhood reflection (and the corresponding sadness) in her "too-compliant, always-eager-to-do-the-right-thing-so-as-not-to-rock-what-she-perceived-to-be-an-already-tenuous-familial-boat" eyes. I should have realized that there is a profound difference between being bright and industrious enough to entertain oneself and the ability to be truly independent, and that in any event, her stated desire to be independent didn't lessen her need to be heard, noticed, and, above all else, to be able to express her feelings and have them validated as an integral member of the family. It also didn't diminish her need for understanding, acceptance, love and affection, even if, like her dad, she wasn't quite sure how to fully accept and embrace them.

Instead, despite having every reason to know better, I think I decided that Ashley was doing great and that I could best contribute to that greatness by simply offering my support and encouragement, certain that if she needed my help with anything—school, extracurricular activities, guys (okay, maybe not guys!), etc., she would ask for it. By doing so, of course, I had unwittingly (and, quite unintentionally) set the stage for her to run headlong into many of the same emotional challenges I had experienced growing up ("On Loneliness and Intimacy"), the ones, paradoxically, that I was so intent on shielding her from. In a very real sense, under what should have been my watchful eye, she truly had become (or was well on her way to becoming) her daddy's little girl—in a few more ways than I had hoped.

Dear Ashley,

Only recently have I begun to realize that in my well-intended efforts to support, encourage and even try to bring healing to you during the course of your illness, I have spent far too much time parenting and coaching and far too little time sharing me. It's not as if I haven't had opportunities to be vulnerable to you—I have. Rather, it's that I haven't always fully embraced them.

I'm thinking, particularly, about a dinner you and I shared a few years back at the window table at Sole. I vividly remember you wondering aloud: "Dad, why don't I have any [true] friends? Why does no one seem to love me for who I am?" I listened in silence—not quite sure of what I should say, if anything, and, ironically, intent on not trying to draw comparisons between what you were feeling and my own adolescence for fear that you might misconstrue my efforts to be empathetic and understanding as my wanting to talk about me.

In the end, all I could say in response was that I had no explanation, that you were (and still are) the most remarkable person I have ever known and that I would have loved to have had a friend like you when I was growing up and trying desperately to find my way in this world. My words were mostly inadequate, an opportunity lost—an opportunity to tell you that, as you were speaking, my heart was breaking for you, because I knew intimately the lonely place from which you were crying out.

I know what it's like to feel as if you're always the one reaching out, the one taking the initiative to garner others' affection, the one having to try too hard—and the profound emptiness that follows when those efforts aren't reciprocated or, worse yet, are abused or taken advantage of. I also know what it's like to long for someone to want and need you simply for who you are and all you have to give. Most importantly, I know the void created when it seems like that person may never come along, particularly in the heart of someone who, like you that night and like me before you, already was questioning whether their uniqueness somehow makes them uniquely "unlovable."

What I didn't know was whether or how to share those things with you that night. I realize now, I should have. I also should have reminded you, as I have tried to do many times since, that, lest there be any doubt in your mind, everything about you, including the things that make you most unique, are precisely what make me love you as much as I do and always will.

With All My Love,
Dad

CHAPTER 3

Brittany

(Living in an "if you ain't first, you're last" world)

*I*n the strangely popular 2006 satirical comedy, *Talladega Nights—The Ballad of Ricky Bobby*, Reese Bobby, a semi-professional stock car driver and full-time alcoholic, makes an unexpected cameo appearance at Career Day in the 5th grade class of his ten-year-old son, Ricky, whom he hasn't seen in years. While smoking a cigarette, Bobby implores his son and his young classmates to disregard their teacher, and as he's being dragged kicking and screaming out the front door by school security, encourages them instead to live by his own personal credo. "Remember, if you ain't first, you're last!" Ricky blindly adopts his dad's advice, and in its pursuit, lives a sometimes hysterical, but always highly dysfunctional life, only later to be told by his dad that he never intended for his impressionable son to take his ramblings seriously.

Regrettably, however, Reese Bobby's mantra reverberates throughout classrooms, playgrounds and boardrooms across the United States with disturbing regularity. Teachers and school administrators, often prompted by equally well-meaning parents, can't seem to label children early enough, advance their studies fast enough, or assign enough homework—to meet what they perceive to be the demands of an increasingly global marketplace. From their perspective, students, particularly those who are deemed to be "gifted" at an early age, need to constantly push the envelope where their studies and extracurricular activities are concerned, in order to create the perfect résumé, the one that will maximize their chances of getting into the best universities and, ultimately, of securing the highest paying and most competitive jobs that our country and the world at large have to offer.

The same troubling mindset also infects our neighborhood and school playgrounds, sports facilities and recital halls, where parents enroll children in a wide range of activities, often at a very early age, in the hope that they will find an activity outside of the classroom that will allow their children to further distinguish themselves from their peers. Many believe that if their children are lucky enough, eventually these activities will earn them a scholarship, or better yet, a career as a professional in their field of choice. Indeed, a plethora of highly structured programs have sprung up over the last several years, all of which cater to the belief that with the right amount of coaching and the requisite investment of time and money, no dream is out of reach, no matter how marginally talented a young man or woman may appear to be in their "chosen" sport or activity at any particular point in time.

Nowhere, however, is Reese Bobby's life view more prevalent than in the workplace, where, from the point at which new employees are hired until the time they are promoted, relegated indefinitely or permanently to their perceived rung on the corporate ladder or shown the door, the individual is evaluated and therefore motivated by an "if you ain't first, you're last" yardstick. By that point, the individual has lived in the shadow of that competitive reality most of their academic and extra-curricular lives, so it doesn't come as a shock. Indeed, we've been groomed to expect that our self-worth will constantly be evaluated based on our ability to be first—first to the office, first with a new idea, first with a solution to a problem someone else created (usually the boss!) while, at the same time willingly be the last to leave the office at the end of the day.

Somewhere along the way, of course, we suffocate the individual, and in the process, deny ourselves and our children the fullness of life that I believe we were all intended to experience. I suppose I'm as guilty of that as the next person, both with respect to my own life, and despite my best efforts, in the lives of my remarkable children, both of whom at a very early age excelled inside and outside of the classroom. I will be the first to admit, looking back, that I missed a number of road signs along the way that, in retrospect, were intended to reveal this fundamental reality to me where my own life and the lives of my children were concerned. Markers that said: "I need (or want) to slow down," to "catch my breath," to "take a break," to "look at what I'm doing here, why I'm doing it and where I'm going," to "decide whether what I'm doing and where I'm going are really what I want to do and where I want to go." Recently, however, that message was delivered to me again, this time through a beautiful young stranger named Brittany (whom you will meet momentarily) and her "Reese Bobby wannabe" father.

Dear Ashley,

I always enjoy going up to our local park on Saturday mornings, not only for the exercise, but for the insights I seem to gain every time I'm there. A recent visit was no exception. As I came around the curve that leads from the parking lot to the path along 152ⁿᵈ Street, I encountered a frenzy of activity on the makeshift soccer fields next to the tennis courts that Saturday mornings always bring. Mothers were busy unloading and setting up their "too much stuff" (e.g., strollers, playpens, duffle bags, coolers, etc.) from the mini-vans/SUVs du jour, while their husbands and smartly dressed 5- and 6-year-old sons and daughters warmed up for the big game.

On the second field down, the coaches had their players running laps around the field to limber up the old muscles. My immediate thought, of course, was that those roles should have been reversed (that the kids should have had their dads running laps—a visual that amused me for a moment). One of the girls, a beautiful and obviously energetic, pigtail-wagging blonde named Brittany, was jogging along at her own pace, admittedly falling a bit behind her already way-too-intense male teammates.

Seeing this, her dad screamed out across the field: "Brittany, pick it up, everybody's beating you!" She immediately responded, shifted into another gear and proceeded to outrun everyone on the field. But there was a price to be paid for her success that her dad completely missed. You see, before her father screamed at her, Brittany didn't even realize, let alone care, that everybody was beating her. She didn't even know it was a race! And she was right—it wasn't.

Brittany was just doing her thing at precisely the pace she wanted to do it. How do I know that? I know because I saw the radiant and carefree smile on her face, the one that said "I'm glad to be alive, I love to run, I love to be at the park" and maybe even "I can't wait for this silly game to start so that I can show these boys a thing or two about playing soccer." I know that because I saw how dramatically that facial expression changed when her dad unknowingly expressed his disappointment in her performance.

I paused for a moment and thought of the number of times that, in spite of my best efforts, you and your brother received similar spoken and unspoken messages from me along the way—

looks of incredulity, frustration or disappointment from dad, when you acted in a way that I never would have expected you to act or failed to perform at a level that I had come to expect of you, and sarcastic comments when you made mistakes and attempted to apologize that almost certainly were taken literally at times ("Don't be sorry, just don't do it!"). I'm also sure that there were times when I was far less subtle in my spoken and written criticisms and admonitions.

But the truth is, I'm the one who's sorry, Ashley—sorry for all the times I failed to reflect the lesson that Brittany and her dad so dramatically and eloquently reminded me of on that soccer field today: Life is not about who is or isn't beating you to the non-existent finish line. It's about finding a pace that brings a smile to your face and learning to ignore the voices that seek to knock you off your stride.

With All My Love,
Dad

CHAPTER 4

The Girl at Detroit Metropolitan Airport

(Turning a deaf ear to the sometimes silent, sometimes not-so-silent tears of those we love)

There is an ever-increasing body of medical and scientific literature which suggests that, over time, children, adolescents and even adults who are repeatedly exposed to violence, even in the form of graphic video games, can become so desensitized to violence in the real world that, at times, they engage in violent behaviors toward family members, friends and strangers alike without any apparent appreciation for the human consequences of their actions.

I often wonder whether the same emotional and psychological principles apply, albeit in much more subtle ways, to other aspects of our lives, including parenting. For example, it seems to me that part of what makes parenting immediately challenging for all and overwhelming for many are the cries of a newborn infant, particularly when it is a first child. An infant's inability to communicate his/her needs except through tears and piercing screams, often in the middle of the night, almost universally evokes a "we've got to fix it" response that leaves many new parents scrambling to guess at what's wrong (*e.g.,* Is the baby sick? Does she need her diaper changed? Is she hungry? Does she need a bottle? Is she tired? Too cold? Too hot? Am I doing something wrong?) so that they can quickly alleviate the tears and restore peace and quiet to their (and the baby's) lives. Unfortunately, new parents seldom guess right the first time (or the second), which often leads to impatience, anxiety, frustration and anger. Suffice it to say, this process, which sometimes is played out innumerable times a day, can be emotionally exhausting.

I can't help but think that, perhaps as a sanity defense mechanism, some parents become somewhat desensitized to those tears and cries for help over time, in part, because they start to figure out that: (1) their child isn't likely to suffer permanent physical or psychological injury if they don't immediately jump to his/her aid; and (2) more often than not, the episode will run its course and resolve itself in the same amount of time regardless of the immediacy of their response or the level of focused energy that they devote to its resolution.

I suspect that while it obviously is not nearly this simple, the eventual desensitization that accompanies this realization helps to explain how parents can sit in a crowded restaurant or airplane and be seemingly oblivious to the screams and tantrums of young children seated right next to them—behavior that is making everyone else visibly uncomfortable. It also likely accounts, in part, for the fact that in their infancy, the siblings that follow the first-born seldom receive the same Pavlovian parental response to every utterance, scream or teardrop that emanates from their equally needy lips, though many other factors undoubtedly also play a role (*e.g.,* the need to suddenly divide a limited pool of parental energy to more than one child, the additional responsibilities of providing for a larger family, the strains that those responsibilities sometimes place on the relationship of the parents themselves, etc.).

Regrettably, however, I suspect that on some subconscious level, that desensitization continues as the child moves into adolescence and young adulthood, even as the child's tears and cries for help persist, often in ways that are just as difficult to interpret as those of a newborn infant, and the sources of those tears grow increasingly complex.

The truth is that we are called to be attentive and responsive to the needs and cries of others, particularly those who we are blessed to call our children. Indeed, in some instances, as parents, the ramifications of not doing so are profound and, at the risk of sounding a bit dramatic, potentially life-threatening.

Dear Ashley,

This afternoon, I was walking through Detroit Metropolitan Airport, en route home from a meeting with a client, when I saw a beautiful young girl with dark curly hair who couldn't have been any more than 5-years-old walking alongside her dad, with tears streaming down her face. I'm not sure why this fairly commonplace airport occurrence captured my attention (I certainly had lots of other "more important" things on my mind), but it did. Maybe it was because there was no apparent reason for the little girl's obvious despair. It wasn't as if she was aggravated by her inability to keep up with her dad, as young children often are in the frantic family footrace from a delayed flight at one end of the terminal to an on-time departure at the other. To the contrary, daughter and dad were walking, albeit distant from one another in other more subtle ways, at a very leisurely pace. I also didn't witness any event that might explain her tears (e.g., a fall, a disciplinary scolding, a "love tap" on the rear, etc.). Maybe it was because, in the midst of his little girl's tears of sadness, her dad couldn't possibly have seemed any less interested.

Later, as I settled into my too-cramped middle seat for the plane ride home, I reflected upon what I had seen and wondered if the tears that littered the concourse floor had come from the little girl having just left her mom at the security check point. Maybe this was her week with her out-of-town dad, who, but for a sense of obligation, would just as soon not be reminded of the marriage he had long since left in his rearview mirror. Or perhaps it wasn't nearly that complicated… maybe she was just having a bad day or was afraid of flying. The point is: it really didn't matter WHY she was crying; what mattered was that she WAS crying and that her dad, for whatever reason, was oblivious or, worse yet, indifferent to her tears.

And then, I started to wonder. I wondered how many times in your young and not-so-young life, I was that dad—how many times I could have but didn't notice and try to dry your tears, shed openly, as that little girl's, or in the privacy of your room, because I was distracted, indifferent, dismissive or simply absent.

I know there must have been lots of those times, Ashley, and I'm truly sorry for each and every one of them.

With All My Love,
Dad

CHAPTER 5

The Gift of Imperfection

(Maybe being perfect isn't all it's cracked up to be)

One truth that is fundamental to the human condition is that all of us are imperfect. And yet, at a very early age, many of us develop a belief that perfection is fully attainable. Regrettably, there are a number of institutions and forces in society that, at every stage of our development, seek to reinforce and promote this truly misguided and often destructive belief. The most obvious examples, of course, are found in the classroom, where perfection is rewarded not simply with an "A"—a grade typically bestowed upon those whose work falls within a range between 93 and 99—but with a 100% —"A+"! In the minds and through the eyes of a student who sees an "A" as often as a blind squirrel stumbles upon a nut, this is a distinction without a difference. They are ecstatic with anything even approaching an "A".

But, to the perfectionist mind, it is one of the earliest indicators that human perfection is real and attainable through hard work—a belief often reinforced by well-meaning parents who, perhaps as a result of their own upbringings or Type A tendencies, tend to focus more on the reason their child missed one question on a ten-question test than on applauding the 9 questions he or she managed to answer correctly.

It is not long before the seeds of perfectionism fully take root and spread to other aspects of our everyday lives. Often, in adolescence and young adulthood, they spill over onto fields of play, stages of artistic expression, and sporting venues, where, in the perfectionist mind, the joy of competition and sense of pride and accomplishment that are intended to accompany the sharing of one's athletic and artistic abilities frequently are supplanted by an overwhelming belief that every performance must be perfect. Typically, what follows when the reality of a poor or imperfect performance occurs, as it inevitably does, is an explosive temper, debilitating feelings of inadequacy, an inability to acknowledge and congratulate others who demonstrate superiority, or worse yet, a propensity to openly criticize other laudable performances, while silently but no less intensely criticizing their own.

Tragically, even on those occasions when perfectionists excel at a given task, as they often do, their sense of fulfillment and enjoyment is short-lived. Instead, seemingly in an instant, their perfectionist mind convinces itself that the day's achievement really wasn't all that big a deal and quickly raises the bar to a new standard of excellence that must be achieved if they are to truly demonstrate to the world just how perfect they can be. Almost unconsciously, their life's journey becomes that of the greyhound, feverishly but futilely pursuing the electronic rabbit (in this case perfection) with no real hope of ever capturing it.

Invariably, before long, the hyper-critical eye of the perfectionist's mind shifts its focus inward, away from the individual's actions and toward the individual herself. Regrettably, what follows is a titanic battle between an often deeply sensitive and compassionate but already tortured soul that longs for a respite from the exhausting quest for external perfection and a mind hell-bent on inflicting even more abuse through a wholesale attack on the face in the mirror. Not surprisingly, the reflection almost never meets the demands of its critic. It is the wrong shape, the wrong size, the wrong skin tone. The complexion is flawed, the body oddly disproportionate, the arms or legs too short or too long, the feet and hands too big or too small. The eyes are too close together, too far apart, the wrong color, the right color, but the wrong shade. The teeth are too big, too small, too close together, not white enough, crooked—and the hair, OH THE HAIR!?! In the end, of course, it is mostly, if not entirely, a gross distortion of the image of the individual seen by the rest of the world, but, to the perfectionist mind, it is very real, and if left unchecked, can threaten the very existence of the perfectionist.

What we fail to realize, despite the fact that, in our daily lives, we repeatedly are confronted with our many shortcomings, is that, paradoxically, the gift of imperfection can be far more liberating than the belief that we are, can or need to be perfect! Indeed, it is the recognition that we are human and fallible that often creates the need and desire for a relationship with God. The realization and acceptance of our imperfection is also what enables us to take chances in life, cognizant of, but not paralyzed by, the reality that things might not work out the way we hoped they would or might not work out at all. Being and recognizing that we are imperfect also makes us more willing to reach out to others who are more skilled in areas where we are, dare I say it, deficient, while simultaneously promoting an increased willingness in us to humbly share our own gifts with others—both life-giving and life-affirming events. Finally and perhaps most importantly, embracing our own imperfections also prompts us to seek the forgiveness of those we have hurt, while at the same time being more willing to forgive those, who in their own imperfection and, likely without any ill intent, have fallen short of our expectations and/or hurt us.

Plainly, if God had intended us to be perfect, He could have done it. The fact that He chose not to was not an accident, let alone a form of punishment, but rather, I suspect, to give all of us greater empathy for others' faults, while sparing us the exhausting and anxiety-producing burden of struggling to achieve the unachievable—perfection.

Dear Ashley,

When I was a boy, I always thought my dad expected me to be perfect. Don't get me wrong; he never actually came out and said that's what he expected—it was just a sense I had. Sometimes the message was subtle. I would come home from school with a B, having worked very hard to get it, only to have my dad question me about what I had missed and why I had missed it, the inference being that I could and should have done better.

Other times, the message was not so subtle. I remember missing shots at a key moment in a bowling tournament and turning around to see my dad with a look of disbelief, what I interpreted as obvious disappointment, or, in some cases, disgust on his face, even though the missed shot may have meant that I finished second or third, instead of first, in a particular tournament. I have similar memories of striking out (which, by the way, I did quite often) or of making errors "at the wrong time" in youth league baseball games and of missing crucial shots in high school and other golf tournaments.

Though the settings may have been different, however, the feelings they elicited were always the same—no matter how well I did or how hard I tried, if, in the end, I wasn't perfect, I felt like my dad was disappointed in me, that I somehow not only let myself down, but I had let him down as well, and it hurt. Often, it hurt a lot because I was no different from most other kids—I hungered for my parents' approval, particularly my dad's. I wanted him to be proud of me. Over time, the inevitable happened: I insisted on perfection in everything I did, and I never seemed to be satisfied

with anything less. I became intolerant of my own and others'
mistakes and shortcomings. I developed a really bad temper and
a really bad attitude whenever I competed at anything and lost.
I also struggled to acknowledge and congratulate others on their
accomplishments and successes, even when they clearly deserved
and had earned my and others' praise. And then I grew to hate
that part of me.

As I grew older (much older, in fact), I began to understand
that there was no way I could ever live up to my dad's expectations
of me or the expectations I had begun to place on myself, because
I never was, am not, and never will be perfect. I also learned that
my dad only wanted me to be the best I could be at the things
I chose to do, and more importantly, that he probably never
realized that the way he chose (or, more likely, had learned from
his own upbringing) to accomplish that goal (i.e., by insisting on
perfection rather than acknowledging and encouraging my small
victories) was hurtful. Finally, I learned that there is much to be
gained and learned from not being perfect, from losing, and from
being vulnerable just like even the most accomplished of people,
performers and athletes are from time to time. It's all part of the
journey, and at the end of the day, these are the experiences from
which we can most grow and become stronger.

And then God blessed me with you and your brother, and
I promised myself that things would be different for you, that I
would always strive to be encouraging, that wherever possible,
I would avoid unwarranted spoken or unspoken criticism, that
I would steadfastly avoid setting standards for you that were
unrealistic or unattainable, that I would teach you the importance
of always being prepared and striving to do your best without
making you feel that I (or anyone else) expected you to be perfect
or that anything less than victory or complete success meant that

you had failed, or worse yet, would result in my thinking any less of you as a person.

I hope that most of the time I've been true to that promise, but knowing how much I still tend to expect of myself and others, often in your presence, I can't help but wonder whether sometimes you feel the same way I did as a child, and it scares me. That fear is the reason I feel compelled to write this note. Don't get me wrong, I want you to strive to do well and make the most of the gifts with which you have been so richly blessed. But I also want you to understand and experience the sense of joy, satisfaction, pride, and accomplishment that comes from knowing you've tried your best, even though, on a given day, your best may not be good enough to achieve the result you had hoped for or thought you deserved.

Most importantly, I want you to know that doing your best and trying your hardest is all that you can reasonably expect from yourself and all Mom and I can reasonably expect of you. No one is perfect in our home, and the good news is that no one ever will be!

With All My Love,

Dad

CHAPTER 6

Dr. Mac

(The value of trust)

*E*arly on in our daughter's illness, at the suggestion of one of her many treating physicians, I reached out to a prominent doctor who heads a hospital-based program in California that is nationally renowned for its work in the treatment of children with eating disorders. Candidly, Dr. Mac had no reason to take my call. My daughter was not in his care and we had never spoken before. But he did take my call. In fact, from the minute he picked up the phone until we hung up nearly an hour later, he was warm and compassionate, empathetic and deeply concerned. He knew the power of the enemy we were dealing with and the difficult path that lay ahead for my daughter and those who loved her.

Dr. Mac provided much wise and practical counsel during that first call and the increasingly desperate calls that followed over the next several weeks. Most importantly, despite his incredibly full plate, he always found the time to listen. One day, he said, "Don, who is the one person Ashley trusts more than anyone in the world?"

"I'm not sure," I replied, having never considered that question before. "I'll have to give it some thought. Why do you ask?"

He paused for a moment and said, "Because my experience has been that he or she is the person who will lead your daughter out of her eating disorder."

I didn't fully grasp the significance or power behind Dr. Mac's statement at the time. The truth is, I was a bit confused by it. But, looking back on the course of Ashley's illness and the countless hours spent in individual and group sessions listening to the stories of other similarly afflicted women of all ages, I think I understand it now. In fact, I am convinced that his message, though important to a better understanding of eating disorders and the journey to recovery, has profound ramifications that transcend eating disorder treatment and is an indispensable ingredient of everyday life.

My sense is that we grossly under-appreciate the importance and power of trust, particularly in the lives of children and young adults. All of us want—indeed need—to be able to trust others. It is an integral part of what allows us to be vulnerable with other human beings. Without trust, it is impossible to feel safe being who we are and to express our innermost feelings honestly without fear of being judged, let alone ridiculed, or worse yet, abandoned. Trust is also what enables us to know that there is someone in the world we can depend upon, unconditionally, someone we can count on to always speak the truth in love where we are concerned—with due respect for us and our feelings.

As children, we are quick to trust, especially those closest to us. More often than not, those people safeguard and nurture that trust because they understand its criticality in our development and in the successful functioning of the family unit. It is no surprise then that, initially, we enter adolescence with a certain naiveté where trust is concerned and readily place our trust in classmates, neighborhood friends, teammates, and even casual acquaintances. We believe, based on our childhood experiences, that our trust will be received with the same respect and safeguarded with the same degree of vigilance that, hopefully, we had grown accustomed to in our home. Too often, however, it is not. In some cases, it is because those in whom we place our trust simply don't assign the value to our gift that it deserves, and in their indifference, violate it. In other cases, those who receive our trust intentionally abuse it for their own selfish benefit.

Regardless of the abuser's intent or lack of intent in violating our trust, however, the results are nearly always the same. With each violation, we become increasingly more reluctant to trust and be open. If it happens often enough (or if a singular violation is particularly severe), we may even begin to second-guess ourselves, our judgment, and ultimately, our very self-worth. Despite the fact that, in most instances, we are wholly innocent victims of others' careless or intentional disregard of our most fundamental and precious gift (our trust), we convince ourselves that there must be something wrong with us, something that makes others unwilling or unable to accept and respect us for who we are.

Predictably, we turn inward, believing that the only person we can truly depend on is ourselves. We become isolated and alone. It is precisely the opening an eating disorder needs to move in and set up its little shop of horrors. Playing off the insecurities that breaches of trust have left behind, the ED voice slowly convinces the starved mind and shame-filled soul that it is the only one worthy of their trust, that it will not abandon them like so many others have before, and all it asks in return is that its host, in turn, trust it implicitly and remain fiercely loyal to it and its directives. Before long, an inseparable bond is formed, a sick and highly dysfunctional distortion of the trust relationship the sufferer always longed for, but, often inexplicably, never found.

Eating disorder treatment facilities are filled with women whose trust was violated—often in profound and unspeakably hurtful ways. Their stories are heart-wrenching. Some were victims of physical and/or sexual abuse by family members beginning at an early age, long before they even had a fighting chance to experience or formulate an understanding of what healthy trust is supposed to look and feel like. Others successfully made it into adolescence or young adulthood with a reasonably healthy sense of and appreciation for the value of trust only to become victims of sexual assault or abuse by a peer who professed to love and respect them. Still others experienced much more subtle, but no less life-altering, violations of their trust through acts of abandonment, betrayal, insensitivity, deceit or simple indifference. For all of these women, the message was the same: "The 'gift of me' that my trust represents is not as valuable as I first thought."

It is impossible to quantify the impact of that message on an individual's psyche. Suffice it to say, violations of trust and the resulting belief that people, even loved ones, can no longer be trusted leaves a brokenness that must be healed if the sufferer is to have any real hope of fully committing to the recovery journey. Part of that healing, certainly the piece that involves dealing with the wounds of the past, is properly left to the treating physician and counselor.

However, parents and loved ones play an equally critical role, not only in addressing trust issues going forward, but, more importantly, in being sensitive to the power of trust in a child's life, before problems relating to its absence or breaches become an issue.

Dear Ashley,

Trust… It's never been an easy thing for either one of us. But there was a time, not so long ago, when you were willing and able to trust. I was too. That desire is still in you (and, I hope, in me as well)!

And, if the sense of excitement, adventure, anticipation, enthusiasm (okay maybe just a LITTLE fear?!?) and imminent joy I see depicted in this photograph—my favorite one of all time—is any indication of its power in your life, it just might be worth rediscovering.

Jump! ... I'll catch you.

With All My Love,

Dad

The Fear

CHAPTER 7

Timothy

(The paralyzing power of fear—An overview)

*I*n his 1993 best seller, *The Twelfth Angel*, Og Mandino introduced the world to Timothy Noble, an impishly small, but infinitely wise and courageous 11-year-old boy. The setting was the youth league baseball try-outs in the small town of Boland, New Hampshire. Also in attendance at the try-outs was John Harding, a hometown hero who, together with his wife, Sally, and their soon-to-be 8-year-old son, Rick, had only recently returned to Boland to settle down and begin John's tenure as the President and CEO of Millennium International, one of the largest computer companies in the country.

Several weeks earlier, Boland had welcomed their "favorite son" and his family home with a parade down Main Street that culminated in the presentation of a special medal honoring John's many personal and professional accomplishments. In presenting the medal, one of Boland's three town Councilmen, retired Judge Thomas Duffy, reminded the thousands who had gathered that, long before he had become Millennium's President, John had been an exceptional youth league, high school and college baseball star (a two-time All-American) who, but for a serious knee injury, almost certainly would have had a very promising major league career.

Tragically, however, with the din of the admiring crowd's celebratory applause still fresh in the Boland air, Sally and Rick were killed in a violent automobile accident. John was devastated. In an instant, the two people he loved more than life itself were gone. Overcome with grief, John took a leave of absence from Millennium and isolated himself in his home, shunning the outside world.

Ultimately, John's despair and loneliness became too great to bear. He contemplated taking his own life. Truth be told, John likely would have "succeeded" had a childhood friend and former youth league teammate, Bill West, not first convinced him to step out of the darkness and emptiness of his living room and use his time away from Millennium to help Bill coach one of Boland's six youth league teams—the Angels.

Enter Timothy Noble… a small, seemingly hopelessly unco-ordinated young boy with an awkward gait, a tattered glove and a heart of gold. Not surprisingly, Timothy was the last person chosen in the draft—the twelfth member of the Angels. What no one (except Timothy, his mother and a very compassionate local doctor) knew at the time—and what John would not discover until long after the Angels' season had ended—was that Timothy was suffering from a terminal illness, an inoperable brain tumor that significantly impaired his vision, balance and coordination. In fact, in many important respects, Timothy was a miniaturized version of John, someone who had every reason in the world not to want to get out of bed in the morning, except for one important difference: Timothy's mind was fixed on a goal. He was intent on playing youth league baseball, and more specifically, on getting a hit in a youth league game, and he was not about to let his illness or the physical limitations it imposed on him get in the way of achieving that goal.

Time and time again, often when the outcome of a game hung in the balance, Timothy failed in the field and at the plate. Incredibly, however, his struggles and disappointments did little to diminish his resolve. If anything, they made him more determined to succeed. Timothy's exuberant and contagious "never, never, never give up" attitude quickly spread to his teammates and became the Angels' rallying cry in what turned out to be a truly magical season, not only for the team and its bravest member, but just as importantly for their coach, John Harding.

As the season wore on, John grew to love Timothy and began working with him before and after practice to try and improve his fielding and hitting skills. His patience and Timothy's hard work paid off. Before long, Timothy was making contact at the plate and sometimes game-saving catches in right field. In his own words, "day by day, in every way [Timothy and John] were getting better and better."

Then, in the final game of the season, with the tying run at third base and his Angel teammates standing as one on the top step of the dugout, it happened—Timothy hit a sharp ground-ball between the first and second basemen. Before the dust settled, Timothy was standing safely on first base, cap in hand, with a smile as big as his heart! His lifelong dream had been realized, and in the process, John was awakened to the realization that he had put the enjoyment of his own life's dream (to be President of Millennium) on hold long enough.

Mandino's message is a clear one with inescapable Biblical roots. At some point, John and Timothy, not knowing each other, let alone what each of their seemingly bleak futures truly held in store for them, had to make a choice. With prayers said, they had to "get up" in faith, step into the light and create an opportunity for God to work not only in their lives, but through them, in the lives of each other. No amount of prayer in the face of inaction was going to equip Timothy with the skill he needed to get his dream hit or to make a game-saving catch, nor would It have enabled John to return to the boardroom with the realization that, despite the unimaginable heartache that accompanied the loss of his wife and only child, he still had much to experience and to give to others.

Their story is a critical point of reflection for all of us, but particularly for those afflicted with physical or emotional illnesses and/ or addictions that, paradoxically, make the darkness and isolation of bed and inaction seem like the most attractive, if not the only, viable option. Too often, I suspect, the pillows in those beds are soaked with tears shed during countless hours of prayers, by those who, out of fear, anxiety, or emotional paralysis then sit and wait for God's answer to descend upon them without their having to do anything. Regrettably, when that doesn't happen, as in the case of Timothy and John it almost certainly would not have had they not left the confines of their home, the afflicted become even more disheartened, believing that God either is not listening to them, doesn't care, or worse yet, has abandoned them to a life of misery. Nothing, of course, could be further from the truth. Timothy taught John (and is there to teach all who will listen) that prayer without some accompanying action, taken in faith, likely is an opportunity for growth—lost.

Dear Ashley,

From the time I was a little boy until well into young adulthood, my parents never made any real effort to shield me (or my brother and sister) from the myriad emotions and challenges that were an integral part of growing up. They also seldom, if ever, took the initiative to comfort, console or empathize with us, when those emotions and challenges became overwhelming, at times even crippling, let alone introduce the possibility that a brighter, happier, more peaceful time awaited us on the other side of a good night's sleep.

Don't get me wrong. I don't believe there was any ill-will behind their actions or inactions, nor do I believe they emanated from the belief that, in essentially leaving us emotional orphans to deal with such things on our own, they would somehow make us more independent or harden us to the point that, as adults, we would be able to deal with any adversity that might come our way. Instead, it is far more likely that their seeming indifference was a by-product of their own Depression-era childhoods or their stumbling in the dark, like most parents, in search of an "Owner's Manual for Children" only to come up empty-handed or, worse yet, with a copy of Dr. Spock's 1946 classic—"The Common Sense Book of Baby and Child Care."

Regardless of their rationale or motives, however, the effect of their parenting techniques on all of us was the same: none of us dared approach our mom and dad with anything about our lives that truly mattered at the risk that our fears, our loneliness, our insecurities would be met with indifference or an admonition that we "deal with it just like all the other kids."

I'm sure, looking back, that those experiences had a lot to do with the promise I made to myself long before you and your brother were born—a promise that I would be a "different" parent, that I would be steadfast and untiring in meeting what I perceived to be your every need, emotional and otherwise— and I set about doing that, with the best of intentions, in what I only later realized were probably all the wrong ways. More than anything else, I wanted you to be happy, and I thought the best way to ensure that was to micro-manage your life, including, among other things, the activities and people in it, in a way that *minimized the risk that you would experience sadness, anger, pain, bitterness, rejection, disappointment, failure, etc.—in short, anything that threatened your happiness and what I readily perceived to be your beautiful, but delicate, spirit. When tears came and anger was expressed, as inevitably and repeatedly they were, I would quickly seek to dispel them with humor, a new activity, a diversion, something more "positively directed"—something geared toward lightening the mood, making you smile, or at a minimum, restoring familial peace.*

Ironically, of course, each time I sought to prevent you from experiencing those emotions, what I was really doing was sending you the same misguided message I too often heard from my own parents, albeit in a very different way: "Don't bother coming to me if your intent is to share an emotion other than happiness or your latest success story 'cause those are the only things welcome in our home!" Not surprisingly, over time, you responded in precisely the same way I did—by shutting down, by isolating, by seeking other outlets to express yourself and your feelings.

I realize now that, along the way, I did you a terrible disservice. My role was not to shield you from the harms and emotions that are an inescapable part of growing up, of living, of loving, of self-discovery, but rather to equip you with the tools necessary to learn from those experiences—and then, little by little, to let you go, so that you could grow into the person you wanted to be, not the person I wanted or thought you should be.

Just as importantly, I needed to be willing to let you make mistakes and experience the consequences of making them (good and bad) without always rushing in from the sidelines to "try to make things better"—even if it meant seeing you suffer from time to time. I'm not sure I did that enough—in fact, I'm quite sure I didn't—and I apologize for that (part of my own fumblings for that ever-elusive "good parenting manual"). I'll try to be more respectful of your judgment and your ability to make your own choices from here on out, but know this (and take comfort in knowing it): I'm still standing on the sidelines, and while I'll try not to rush out on the field anymore, I promise to be available in case you ever want to call a time-out and chat about what's going on in the game!

With All My Love,
Dad

CHAPTER 8

Travis

(The fear of failure)

Over the years, I have become increasingly aware of a number of invisible barriers that sometimes block what others perceive to be a clear and unobstructed metaphorical pathway between the security of the four walls of our bedroom or homes and the threshold of the door leading to the outside world. Perhaps the most prominent of those barriers is fear. That fear emanates, at least in part, from a belief that the magnitude of the challenges that await us when and if we muster the courage to step across that threshold are simply too complicated, too painful or too overwhelming to tackle.

Fear can take many forms. For many, it is a fear of failure—what will happen if we fall flat on our face and have to retreat back into the darkness? What then? Like most fears, but particularly with the fear of failure, the result is almost always the same—physical and emotional paralysis.

In a perfect world, it is difficult to reconcile fear and anxiety with an abiding faith in a God who is all-loving, all-faithful and all-

46

forgiving. The concepts seem mutually exclusive. Indeed, the Bible repeatedly encourages those of faith to avoid anxiety and fear at every turn – and with good reason: fear and anxiety indisputably are two of the least productive and most destructive emotions that we experience.

Notwithstanding those admonitions, however, and despite our best efforts, it's fair to assume that fear and anxiety will continue to be an integral and expanding part of the human condition. The fact is that we live in an imperfect, increasingly complex, fast-paced, competitive and stressful world. Advances in technology, which, on the drawing board, seemed certain to simplify our daily existence, have done just the opposite. They (particularly the internet and its related gadgets) have made information and images, positive and negative, accessible to the point that it is, at times, overwhelming. As if that weren't enough, all of us, but particularly our children and young adults, are constantly bombarded with voices telling us how we should look, what we should eat and drink, what we should wear and where we should buy it, how much we should exercise, what we should study, where we should live, what job we should have, how many hours we should work, what music we should be listening to, what car we should drive, what movies we are expected to like, what schools we should aspire to attend, and even what success looks like. Adolescents trying to find their way in today's world who take their fingers off that pulse for even a second do so at their own peril, and too often at the risk of social alienation.

All of this, of course, is superimposed on an already full plate of daily activities and demands and, more importantly, the interpersonal struggles that occupy all of our minds (*e.g.,* the need to first accept the person who greets us in the mirror each morning and then find acceptance among peers, the desire to love and be loved, a longing for true friendship, a quest to please and be reaffirmed by our parents, a figuring out of our faith and how to apply it in an increasingly secular world, the question of how we will ever be able to support ourselves, dealing with heartache and heartbreak, worrying about world events that seem to threaten peace and prosperity, etc.). It is hard enough for the uniquely independent, competent and well-adjusted among us to juggle it all and remain healthy—all of the time. Even among that select group, I suspect that a fear of failure and the resulting anxiety figure prominently, and I'm certain they do in the lives and minds of those who, for one reason or another, find themselves completely overwhelmed.

Curiously, the power of the fear of failure was made clear to me on a youth league baseball field many years ago. Every year, the coaches in our local league picked 15 all-stars to play in a countywide, end-of-the-year tournament. Predictably, most of the boys came from the top two teams in the league. But one of them, the team's smallest member, came from a team that had lost its final 11 games and finished in last place. Still, he was the all-star coaches' only unanimous selection—a very talented player who had led our team in hitting and fielding and had become known throughout the league for his fiercely competitive spirit, his constant hustle and his unique ability to bunt. No one who had seen that young boy play that year questioned his right to be an all-star—no one, that is, except the boy himself.

To this day, I'm not sure whether it was the fact that his team had become the laughing-stock of the league, the unkind remarks made by a few of his more successful all-star teammates or simply his size, but from the minute the boy was notified of his selection, he doubted whether he belonged on the same field with the league's best. When the day of the big game finally arrived, the boy's sense of self-doubt and fear of failure was so great that he could barely play. He struck out his first two times up, without the bat even leaving his shoulder, and his two fielding errors in the top of the eighth inning had allowed the visiting team to tie the score. During the regular season, such failures would have forced the young boy to try harder, fired him up, made him all the more eager for one more chance to be a hero. That night, however, there was no fire in the little all-star, only fear and a quiet prayer that he would not get another chance to let his team down.

Things didn't work out quite the way he had hoped. With two outs and the score still tied in the bottom of the eighth, the boy's teammates loaded the bases! He was due up next. But, as he started out of the dugout, he froze, doubled over as if in pain, and tearfully told his coach that he was "too sick to bat." The opposing manager saw the mysterious illness as simply a trick to enable the home team to skip over its weakest player. He immediately protested, insisting that the umpire either force the boy to bat or declare him to be the third and final out. Soon, several of the coaches and parents had joined in the argument at home plate, and within minutes, the little boy, who had long since retreated back into the dugout, wanting only to be left alone, became the center of attention. Having no place else to hide, the little boy buried his face in his hands and cried.

Moments later, the boy's coach during the regular season stuck his hand through the wire mesh fence and tapped the boy on his shoulder. He greeted the boy's face, which was riddled with fear and anxiety, with a gentle and disarming smile. The coach explained to the boy that he had a choice to make: he could either stay on the bench, in which case he was certain to be called out, ending his team's rally, or he could step up to the plate and at least give himself and his team a chance to succeed. "Better yet," he whispered, "you could deliver one of your famous bunts and really create some excitement around here!" The little boy's eyes said it all as he returned his coach's smile. Then, grabbing his helmet and bat and amid a thunderous round of applause, he silenced the ongoing debate at home plate by quietly taking his stance in the batter's box. On the very first pitch, the boy stunned *almost* everyone in the park by laying down a near-perfect bunt! When the dust settled, the little boy was on first base, the pain in his stomach was gone, and what turned out to be the game-winning run had crossed home plate!

The messages of that moment, which are etched in my mind to this day, were simple but no less powerful. First, the uncertainty and the magnitude of the challenges that all of us are asked to confront from time-to-time and the anxiety and fear of failure that they carry with them are real. What is not real, what is a lie, and yet what sometimes keeps us from being able to move forward, is the idea that we have to tackle all of these challenges at once—that (to borrow a baseball analogy) at every turn we need to step up to the plate and knock the challenge or the task at hand "out of the park."

However, the truth is that every journey, short or long, simple or complex, starts with the smallest of first steps (a bunt, if you will); and, lest any of us be concerned, there are many people standing behind us ready to pick us up if we should stumble or fall.

Second, if we aren't willing to get off the bench and at least create an opportunity for success and self-fulfillment, we almost certainly, albeit paradoxically, will realize the thing we fear the most: failure! In the case of our little all-star, had he not crossed the threshold of the dugout, stepped into that batter's box and mustered the courage to square around to bunt, he would have been called out, and his team's rally, indeed, the entire game, would have ended.

Dear Ashley,

I wonder how much you remember about the first (and only) ski trip we took as a family—to Smuggler's Notch in 1997. You were 8 years old at the time. I remember a lot about that trip. I remember we lost our luggage and I spent the first 24 hours going "spider monkey" on every airline representative who had the misfortune of answering the phone, more disturbing "dad fun" for the whole family. I remember it snowing every morning on cue and how beautiful the resort and Burlington looked in its majestic white blanket. I remember dropping you and your brother off at the chair lift that first morning and the enthusiasm and anticipation on your faces. I remember heading off to Bunny Slope School with your mom and feeling like I'd be just fine if I spent the entire week there. I remember watching you and your brother speed down the slopes that second day like you'd been skiing your entire lives. I remember cringing later that morning as your mom screamed at our Bunny Slope professor that she was bored with the speed bump-sized hills we were learning on and insisted that she/we were ready to graduate to the big slopes. I remember feeling much less certain about my skiing acumen than your mom, as I slowly snowplowed down the hill only to hear her bloodcurdling screams behind me as she tore one ligament after another in her first trip down. I remember a bunch of muscle-bound, blonde-haired Big Slope Snow Patrol Dudes whisking her off the slope on a stretcher into the first aide trailer at the bottom of the hill. I remember her spending the rest of the trip on crutches, waiting at the base of the hill in the fireplace-warmed ski lodge for one or more of us to finish our morning runs.

But I also remember that trip for a different, more positive reason. I remember it for what you taught me about fear. It was the day after mom's accident, my first trip back up the mountain that had been the scene of the crime. Do you remember? I had just stumbled out of the chair lift with you and your brother and was standing frozen in place like an ice statue at the top of the hill. The bottom looked a long way away. I was terrified. Apparently, it was pretty obvious because you turned to me and quite matter-of-factly said, "Dad, I think it's time to face your fears!" For an 8-year-old you, likely and properly without a fear in the world, it was just as simple as that. For me, however, filled with a world of fears, not the least of which was that I had seen your mom blow out her knee the day before, it was considerably more complicated. The truth is that I had never done very well when it came to putting things on my feet other than tennis shoes (e.g., ice skates, roller blades, water skis, etc.). In fact, once at a water-skiing outing with several teenage friends, I actually managed to use the back of a surfacing manatee as a ski ramp and went airborne, resulting in one of the wickedest and most embarrassing wipeouts the lake across from Miami International Airport has ever seen. The fact that it came on the heels of my having earlier dropped the slalom ski, rather than its single-booted colleague, in my first and last attempt at slaloming only heightened my sense of humiliation, while simultaneously embedding a fear of anything ski-related for a lifetime.

But, at the end of the day, you were right. What you were really saying is: "Dad, what's the worst that can happen if you just allow that ski tip to drift toward the edge of the slope?" Believe me, I thought about that for a moment. There was chance I could get hurt, maybe even tear a ligament (or two), but the truth is, as long as I was careful, that chance was pretty remote, and even if it did happen, I knew plenty of doctors back in Miami who could put Humpty Dumpty back together again. There also was a chance (a much more likely one) that I could fall flat on my face and in the process risk humiliating myself in front of the hundreds of more accomplished skiers that inhabited the slopes that day—not to mention in front of you and your brother. But the truth was that it was far more likely that you guys (and the other skiers) would get a chuckle out of my ineptness and clumsiness—and I was actually okay with that. In fact, I thought it might be good for you and your brother to see me struggle with something that with just two short days of practice and almost no instruction, both of you already could do so well. And so I set out, and I fell, and you laughed; and I got up, and I fell—and you and your brother sped past and told me you'd catch up with me at the bottom of the hill—and off you went, smiling at your still-trying-to-get-it-right-but-no-longer-fearful-about-skiing dad.

I have you to thank for that moment of clarity about fear, Ashley. Because of it and my corresponding decision not to allow fear to keep me in its paralyzing grip, I actually learned how to ski (well, sort of!) and, most importantly, got to spend the days that followed building unforgettable memories exploring the snow-covered trails of Smuggler's Notch with you and your brother. I've drawn on your words countless times since that December morning 14 years ago and it continues to make a difference in my life.

I think Franklin Delano Roosevelt and my 8-year-old daughter got it right: "There [truly] is nothing to fear, but fear itself!"

With All My Love,
Dad

CHAPTER 9

Junnuh

(The fear that a healthier, happier you
is a distant and irretrievable memory)

*I*n 1917, Rannulph Junnuh was a young man who seemed to have the world on a string. He had a beautiful girlfriend, Adele Invergordon, the daughter of a wealthy Southern landowner, and he was the most gifted golfer in Savannah, Georgia, if not the entire southeastern United States. Then, World War I intervened. Junnuh was summoned to fight in the European theater and, before long, was part of a regiment that was involved in a bloody firefight. The entire regiment, save for Junnuh, was slaughtered. Junnuh was devastated and tormented by the horrific experience. He spent the next 15 years in a self-imposed exile, wallowing in the guilt, shame and self-pity brought on by the trauma. When he finally returned to Savannah in 1930, Junnuh was a shell of the man who had left 15 years earlier.

Savannah, too, was different. The Great Depression had taken its toll on the once-proud city. Adele's father, having lost virtually everything he owned and deeply in debt, had taken his own life. The tax collectors quickly descended on Adele and insisted that she sell the last of her father's properties, a quaint golf course on the outskirts of town, to satisfy his debts. But Adele resisted. Instead, she proposed to bring to Savannah "the greatest golf match ever played"—a $10,000 winner-take-all event between two living legends, Walter Hagen and Bobby Jones—in the hope that the funds it would generate would allow her to save her father's course. The townspeople enthusiastically embraced the idea with one caveat; they insisted that one of their own compete in the match.

The logical choice, of course, was Junnuh. The only problem was that Junnuh, who, upon his return from the war, had dedicated his life to alcohol and carousing with local drifters, wanted nothing to do with it and made his feelings quite clear to Adele.

Fortunately, an innocent young boy named Hardy Greaves, who knew of Junnuh only through the stories he had heard of Junnuh's pre-war golf prowess at his family's dining room table and had grown to idolize him, reached out to Junnuh and implored him to reconsider his decision. Junnuh reluctantly agreed, blew the dust off of his old clubs and began the tedious task of trying to recapture the swing and the game that had made him such an iconic player when he was young.

Suffice it to say, the road back was far more complicated and frustrating than even Junnuh had anticipated, so much so that on more than one occasion, Junnuh decided it simply wasn't worth the effort. As he was about to return to his new life on the streets, Junnuh encountered a unique caddy who offered to help him regain the life and the game he once knew and loved. That caddy's name was Bagger Vance, the central character in what likely was the best movie that no one saw in 2000 (*The Legend of Bagger Vance*). Slowly and patiently, Bagger, who plainly serves as a Divine intervener, reminded Junnuh of his former skills and readied him for the two-day match—or so he thought.

Regrettably, it didn't take long for Junnuh, Bagger, Hardy, or Adele to realize that the demons that had followed Junnuh into exile and drove him to drink and live with the town drifters weren't about to give up their stronghold on his psyche and his spirit without a fight. Indeed, the match had barely started before the memories of that terrible day on the battlefield intruded and began to siphon off what little strength, confidence and determination Bagger had managed to re-instill in Junnuh's soul. By the end of the first day, Junnuh had all but given up the fight and found himself hopelessly behind his legendary competitors.

Day two promised to be much of the same, as Junnuh hit two poor shots for every good one—one of which found its way deep into the woods. What followed was arguably one of the most powerful philosophical scenes in any movie in the last twenty years.

As Junnuh began searching for his errant tee shot in the forest, his mind again flashed back to the sights and sounds of that horrific day in World War I. He could see clearly the carnage of his fellow soldiers and friends strewn about the battlefield as the sound of rifles and heavy artillery reverberated in his head. It was more than he could bear. He desperately wanted to flee, to escape back into hiding, back into the bottle. As Junnuh's trembling hand reached down to pick up his ball, an act which likely would have signaled the end to his comeback effort, Bagger appeared and questioned Junnuh's intentions.

Bagger began by innocently asking Junnuh if he was "gonna be needing another club?" Junnuh's demons quickly rose to his defense. He angrily accused Bagger of not understanding his predicament. From Junnuh's perspective, Bagger not only didn't understand, he couldn't possibly understand. After all, he didn't see the things Junnuh saw. He wasn't forced to confront the terror of war. He hadn't felt the power of that darkness, the void that kept gnawing at his soul, wanting to draw him back in to keep him from remembering who he was before the war. Junnuh's pain was palpable and overwhelming.

At that moment, Bagger revealed himself to Junnuh and Hardy. He patiently but sternly explained that "there isn't a soul on this entire Earth who doesn't have a burden to carry"—a burden they don't and may never understand. Then, in a critical turning point, Bagger gave Junnuh permission to heal, to step out of the darkness, to forgive those who inflicted the suffering on him. He told Junnuh that the time had come to set down his pain, "to play the game that he was given when he came into the world, the game that only he was meant to play." The game Bagger was talking about, of course, had nothing to do with golf and everything to do with life. Bagger's message is powerful—that life, like golf, is a game to be played—not won. It's not about the finish line. It's about the journey.

Bagger astutely sensed that Junnuh desperately wanted to break free from the grip of the demons that seemingly wouldn't let go. Junnuh seemed willing, but confessed to Bagger that he just didn't know how to do what Bagger was asking him to do. In fact, he was convinced "he couldn't" do it. Ultimately, Bagger told Junnuh that he had a choice: he could either stay stuck or strike out for the light, begin walking forward toward the place and person he was before the war, but with a new level of understanding. Junnuh was frightened and uncertain of his ability to let go. He told Bagger "it was just too long ago"—suggesting he could not even remember what life was like before the trauma. Lovingly, Bagger assured him that "it was just a moment ago" and then let him know he was not alone—that he, Bagger, had "been there all along" and that he would continue to be there. Moments later, Junnuh took his grip and stance, and holding nothing back, laced a perfect shot through a narrow sunlit crease in the darkened forest. His journey back to himself had begun.

Junnuh's life experiences are not unlike the experiences of those who find themselves firmly in the grasp of an eating disorder. In many instances, there is a dark event that creates an opening for the ED voice to slither Its way in and take up residence in its unsuspecting victim's mind and suddenly vulnerable soul. Sometimes the event takes the form of trauma. For others, the crack in their emotional and psychological armor emanates from far more subtle events—a breach of trust by a loved one, a moment of profound sadness or self-doubt, a fundamental change in circumstance, a sense that life is spinning hopelessly out of control, etc.

Once it weasels its way in, however, it is only a matter of time before the ED voice begins to isolate the individual from the life-giving and life-affirming people and events that, in a healthier moment, otherwise might have enabled them to bridge the momentary periods of darkness that inevitably are part of all of our life experiences.

Ultimately, the darkness expands, as it did in Junnuh's life, to fully consume and then suffocate the individual's pre-illness identity, leaving the hyper-vigilant and unmercifully critical ED voice fully in control of the dispirited carcass its handiwork has helped to fashion. Day after day, missed meal after missed meal, a bond is formed between the predator and its prey. In the same way that Junnuh identified himself as "someone who had experienced the horrors of war," the eating disorder becomes the disordered eater's identity. It is how they see themselves and, inexplicably, the way they want to be perceived by the outside world. An "us against them" mentality slowly emerges and with it, a sense by the sufferer that those outside the bond simply don't and can't understand. Paradoxically, of course, it is the victims of ED and not their caretakers or loved ones, who, in part, because of the toll starvation takes on the mind, become less and less able to understand the urgency of their predicament.

If the analogy holds true, then the principles Bagger offered Junnuh should be equally applicable to disordered eaters in helping them put the suddenly shuffled pieces of their life's puzzle back together. Critical to that process is identifying someone who the sufferer trusts above all others—their Bagger Vance.

Once identified, that individual must take it upon himself or herself to begin re-introducing their loved one to her pre-illness self, with a particular emphasis on those people, places, things and activities that brought her peace and joy and made her unique—her "game, the one that only [she] was meant to play, the one that [she] was given when she came into this world." With patience, tenderness and unconditional love and support, the trusted one needs to dispel the notion, as Bagger did with Junnuh in the woods, that their loved one's pre-illness self is not some long forgotten, irretrievable memory, but rather a spirit that is still very much alive inside of her, who longs to be set free. The hope and the goal is to provide fertile ground in which the pre-illness self can gain a foothold and begin fighting back against the uninvited intermeddler. This is often a complex and arduous process, but the results are well worth the time and effort.

Dear Ashley,

I went by the hanging rings at the park today—in fact, I passed by them three times. Each time the images became clearer—you playfully swinging from them, a smile from ear to ear, not a care in the world save for how far you could launch yourself in the air with a swinging start. Do you remember? I do. I have lots of memories like that.

It's a relatively simple snapshot I know, but an important one because it depicts a time in your life when you and I had never heard of eating disorders, let alone knew what it meant to restrict, to purge or to engage in other forms of self-harm. Truth is—in what then was (and what will be again) a life and a heart overflowing with dreams, hope, love, and anticipation, there was no room for "Mr. ED."

Obviously, somewhere along the way, he weaseled his way in, and like a bad tenant, immediately started doing things his way—punching holes in the walls, spilling grape juice on the carpet, rearranging the furniture, breaking the lights and light fixtures—in short, doing everything he could to suffocate you and make room for him. One day, however, his gig will be up.

One snack, one meal, one friend, one day at a time, you will decide to evict Mr. ED—once and for all, and when he's gone, you can patch the holes and repaint the walls in any color or colors you choose. You can clean the carpet, bring in bright and beautiful new furniture and put it wherever you would like—and then, once you have things just the way you want them, you can illuminate it all with the radiance of the smile I saw so vividly in my mind this morning.

With All My Love,
Dad

CHAPTER 10

Brock

(The fear that we can't, before we've even tried)

*I*t's not often that you'll find me in the house on a weekend, particularly on a sunny summer Sunday afternoon. I'm sure some of that is a by-product of my childhood. I always loved to be outdoors. It didn't matter how hot or cold it was or what I was doing—playing catch with my brother, riding my bike, playing football with friends, shoveling snow, mowing or trimming the lawn, hitting plastic golf balls to sprinkler heads in the front yard, or spending hours by myself at the driving range and putting green, so long as I wasn't sitting around the house, I was happy.

Part of it also is no doubt attributable to the fact that my chosen profession requires me to spend 90 percent of the daylight hours in my work week in a small air-conditioned office, watching one spectacular day after another pass by through the slats of my mini-blinds.

But on one particular Sunday a few years ago, that is precisely where you would have found me—sprawled out on the sofa, with a glass of iced tea in one hand and the T.V. remote in the other. It was oppressively hot outside, even for my liking, and I had decided, in the vernacular of my kids, to just "chill out" for a minute. Turns out, I don't think my being there was an accident.

As I was flipping through the 600 or 700 mostly useless channels that now populate our modern-day cable packages, I stumbled across what I would later learn was the 2006 film, *Facing the Giants*. In it, Grant Taylor, a sixth-year football coach at a small Christian high school, is faced with the prospect of losing his job if his undersized and, at least from the standpoint of a hardcore group of fathers, underachieving "Shiloh Eagles" once again failed to have a winning season under Taylor's tutelage. To make matters worse, just as the season was about to begin, the Eagles' star senior running back transferred to a cross-town rival. Not surprisingly, the Eagles lost their first three games.

As if all of this were not enough, Taylor's burdens multiplied tenfold when he learned that he and his young wife, Brooke, likely would have to come to grips with the reality that, due to infertility, they would never have children of their own. Confronted with these seemingly insurmountable obstacles all at once and with nowhere else to turn, Taylor looked to God for guidance, and in the midst of his prayers, received a visitor in his office who encouraged him to remain faithful and prepare himself and his team to receive God's blessing.

Inspired, Taylor challenged himself and his players to embrace their God-given talents, to dedicate themselves and the remainder of the Eagles' season to putting those talents on display for His glory, and to entertain with an open mind and heart the idea that by doing so, anything was possible. Suffice it to say, the team and assistant coaches weren't exactly quick to jump on Taylor's newly designed, inspirational bandwagon—that is until an incredible sequence of events that flashed on the screen just a few minutes after my arrival.

It turns out that the team had just completed the "Death Crawl," a diabolical strength and conditioning drill that requires one player to lie "back down" on the back of a teammate, who is then required to balance and carry the player, clinging to his shoulder pads, with only his hands and feet touching the ground, a distance of 10 yards! Not surprisingly, at the 10-yard mark, virtually all of the players relegated to the role of human pack mule collapsed in a heap before gathering back at the goal line for a brief rest. During the good-natured horse-play that followed, one of the team's newest members asked Taylor how strong their next opponent (Westview) was. Without a second thought, the Eagles' defensive captain and supposed team leader, Brock Kelly, blurted out, "A lot stronger than we are!"

Sensing a teachable moment, Taylor called Brock out, asking if he "had already written Friday [night's game] down as a loss." "Not if I knew we could beat'em," Brock replied. Taylor then summoned Brock and his teammate, Jeremy, to the front of the team and told him he wanted to "see him do the Death Crawl again, but this time [Taylor] wanted to see Brock's absolute best." Ever the cocky one, Brock boldly pronounced that he "bet he could go to the 50-yard line with no one on his back." Taylor said, "I think you can go to the 50-yard line with Jeremy on your back, but even if [you can't], I want you to promise me you will give me your best—your very best." Brock shrugged his shoulders and half-heartedly promised he would. Taylor then told Brock there was one more thing: he wanted Brock to do the drill blindfolded! When asked why, Taylor responded, "Because I don't want you giving up at a certain point when you could go farther." And so the exercise began.

It's difficult for words to adequately capture the intensity or the importance of the 3-minute clip that followed. As Brock unknowingly crossed one yardage marker after another, his coach repeatedly exhorted his star in training "not to give up," reassuring him with each step he took that "[he] had more than that [to give]." As the steps grew more difficult and Brock threatened to give up, Taylor's exhortations grew louder and more animated. He implored his young star to keep going, which Brock did before eventually collapsing face down at his coach's feet. Totally spent and in tears, Brock told his coach that "he had to have made It to the 50-yard line." His coach removed the blindfold and asked Brock to look up and see that he was in the opposite end zone, that he had just carried a 160-pound teammate on his back across the entire 100 yard field!

Taylor concluded by telling Brock that God had gifted him with the ability of leadership, and he encouraged him to use that gift (as well as his obvious strength and courage), not only for his own benefit, but for the benefit of his friends and teammates who looked to Brock to set an example for their own behavior and level of commitment. He told Brock that if he allowed his gift of leadership to remain dormant and in its place adopted a defeatist attitude, the team was almost certain to follow.

The confrontation between Taylor and Brock illustrates, in very dramatic fashion, what I believe is a critical reason many of us, particularly those battling eating disorders and other addictive diseases, often struggle to even "get off the couch," let alone take the first step toward the life that I believe all of us were meant to embrace on the other side of the metaphorical front door. Like Brock, we have convinced ourselves long before the game is even played that there is no way we can possibly prevail against the challenges that lie in front of us. To be sure, as was the case with Brock that day on the practice field, there often is plenty of objective evidence to support such a conviction. Indeed, if instead of calling him out, Taylor had pulled Brock aside and simply asked him why, on a Wednesday, he already was putting Friday night's game in the loss column, Brock certainly would have pointed to the fact that the Eagles were off to an 0-3 start and were coming off five consecutive losing seasons. He also likely would have reminded Taylor in case he had forgotten that the Eagles were without their star running back. Finally, Brock might have mentioned the undeniable fact that the team's upcoming opponent was bigger and stronger than the Eagles. In short, Brock could have constructed a compelling and convincing argument that the deck was stacked against the Eagles, much as it often seems to those confronted with the insidiousness of an eating disorder or other addictive diseases.

Taylor certainly wasn't oblivious to those facts, but he also realized and found an opportunity to rather graphically illustrate to Brock and his teammates several fundamental truths that, while perhaps a bit less obvious than their objective counterparts, were equally critical realities for Brock and his teammates to consider in evaluating their chances against their upcoming opponent. First, left to our own devices, particularly when our view of self and others is compromised by disease or simply the baggage of unpleasant life experiences, we will almost always anticipate that a worst case scenario awaits us on the other side of the threshold of the metaphorical front door ("So coach, how strong is Westview this year? A lot stronger than we are!"). For some, this is nothing more than a built-in defense mechanism—we're hedging our bets. If we expect the worst and it materializes, we are likely to be less disappointed, whereas if things don't turn out quite as bad as we expected or, better yet, go great, it heightens our sense of accomplishment and satisfaction. For others, it is a paralyzing thought that results in their remaining firmly planted on the couch.

Second, Taylor understood that, more often than not, we grossly underestimate our physical, emotional and spiritual capacities to overcome whatever obstacles we may encounter on our respective journeys to the goal line. Stated otherwise, like a blindfold-less Brock, we predetermine how far we think we are capable of going or are willing to go and then likely stop just short of or precisely at that point. Taylor knew that if he could instill an opposite voice, one that would enable Brock to experience the power of the gifts of courage and leadership with which he had been so richly blessed, he might be able to dispel the self-doubt that left Brock feeling defeated before the battle even began. To do that, however, Taylor had to first extract a commitment from Brock that "he was prepared to give [Taylor] his best—his absolute best" regardless of where that best ultimately took the two of them—and Brock had to be willing to make that commitment. Next, Taylor had to blindfold Brock so that what his mind and his eyes defined as the limits of his gifts did not supplant their actual limits. Finally, at least for the first 100 yards of Brock's journey, Taylor had to be willing to walk and, at times, crawl right beside him, validating his struggle and his pain, while at the same time encouraging him and coaxing him on. Initially, Taylor's opposite voice was soft and reassuring, a message to his young star that he (Taylor) knew what he was doing and could be trusted to guide Brock. But as the journey grew more difficult and Brock's inner voices of self-doubt and inadequacy began to pour out, Taylor's opposite voice became louder, more emphatic and unequivocal. Ultimately, it served its purpose, drowning out its self-limiting counterpart just long enough for Brock (and his teammates) to catch a glimpse of his true potential, and hopefully, at least from Taylor's perspective, a desire to catch another glimpse, and another, and another.

Dear Ashley,

Believe it or not, some of life's most important messages and fundamental truths are found in children's books. The problem is, we read them as young children (or, more often, have them read to us), think they're cute, toss them aside, and never read them again… after all, they're just children's books, right?!? Wrong.

Take, for example, "The Little Engine That Could" by Watty Piper. The story seems simple enough (perhaps even a bit corny) on *its face—a train delivering toys, stuffed animals, fruits, and other goodies to children who live on the other side of a steep mountain, breaks down unexpectedly several miles short of its destination.*

The animals and toys leap off the train in the hope that a passing engine will see their plight and pull them over the mountain. One by one, powerful steam engines stop, but just long enough to thumb their noses at the desperate toys. Eventually, a tired and rusty engine stops. The reader senses that the old steam engine would like to help, but a lifetime of little disappointments and the self-doubt they left behind have burdened him with an "I can't" mentality that makes it impossible for the train to muster the strength it needs to carry the train over the mountain.

Moments later, a small train happens upon the broken down, toy-laden train. Initially, she's convinced that she will never get over the mountain: "I'm not very big." "They use me only for switching trains in the yard." "I've never been over the mountain." However, the little train eventually summons the courage and the strength to replace her self-doubt with self-confidence (an "I think I can" attitude). With a renewed sense of belief in herself (and a lot of effort), she manages to climb the mountain that, only moments before, seemed insurmountable.

There is an important lesson here for all of us: Second to prayer, the power of positive thinking is the most important weapon you can bring into the battles that you are certain to fight in the classroom, on stage, in the workplace and in relationships for the rest of your life. Ashley, God has blessed you with an incredible mind and a resilient spirit. I encourage you to fill that mind with positive thoughts.

The reality is that I can believe in you and your tremendous gifts and abilities "until the cows come home" (AND I DO!!!), but in the end, my believing won't make enough of a difference unless YOU BELIEVE IN YOURSELF, particularly in the face of adversity, heartache, and disappointment. I hope you enjoy the enclosed copy of The Little Engine That Could and will always remember that silly little blue train whenever you "think you can't."

With All My Love,
Dad

CHAPTER 11

Courtney

(The power of our gifts and the corresponding
fears of success and of disappointing others)

O ver the years, psychologists, philosophers and others have
devoted considerable thought and ink to exploring the fear
of failure—and rightfully so; it is an emotion nearly everyone
has experienced or will experience on some level at some point in their
life. However, I believe there is an equally compelling fear that keeps
many from the fullness of life we are meant to experience, namely
the fear of success. It is the voice within us that asks: "What happens
if I cross the threshold to the outside world and I don't fail?" "What
happens if, as those who believe in and love me most contend, I prove
to be far more capable and competent than my current circumstances
suggest that I am? What happens if I not only confront and prevail
against the challenges I face, but fully embrace and make manifest
the gifts with which I have been entrusted for all of the world to
see? What then? What will the expectation be? Will I have to do it
again (and again)?" "What happens if I have to remain in the light?"

Surprisingly, I suspect this fear is more prevalent than one might think, particularly in those who, often at a very young age, realize that their gifts are unique and potentially powerful—gifts that to a parent, teacher or coach, seem like a blessing that make their possessor wonderfully different from the overwhelming majority of their peers and potentially great, but that, to their possessor, may, at times, seem more like a burden.

I always sensed that this fear existed, but the reality and potentially disabling power of it didn't become clear to me until a few years ago, when, at a quiet dinner, I asked a young friend who had always excelled in the classroom and on the stage as a ballerina whether she had ever experienced those emotions and, if so, what impact they had on her and, most importantly, how did she ultimately manage to overcome them. She smiled, wondering, I suspect, why someone had never asked her those questions before, and then, as if relieved to finally be sharing the truth (and secrets) of her journey, offered the following reflections:

"My experiences with the fear of success began in the classroom, at a very early age. From the time I was very young, I realized I was pretty smart. School, like dance, came naturally to me. Before long, all of the teachers in the school, as well as my classmates, knew me and my reputation for academic excellence (*e.g.,* "She's brilliant. You're going to love having her in your class," "Courtney will show you. She's the fastest learner;" "Ask Courtney; she's always right"). They talked me up so much that whenever I entered a new grade or was introduced to a new subject like chemistry or calculus, the teachers expected me to quickly grasp the material and excel on my exams and papers—and I usually did, thanks to a lot more hard work than most of my peers probably realized. I knew exactly what was expected of me, based on my past performances, and I began to feel a tremendous amount of anxiety in having to constantly repeat, if not improve upon them. I distinctly recall feelings of dread and intimidation every time I heard a new teacher explain his/her policies and the class syllabus for the first time. I never thought to simply trust my ability to learn and allow that I might not understand certain subjects so quickly. In the end, none of my elementary, middle or high school courses ever got the best of me. As each year passed, my mostly unblemished report card remained intact, but my continued successes only served to fuel what, unbeknownst to even those closest to me, was becoming an increasingly uncontrollable fear that I was expected to succeed at everything or risk disappointing my parents and everyone else who believed in me.

Not surprisingly, those same fears spilled over onto the dance floor. For as long as I can remember, I've always loved to dance. It is and always has been my passion, and, as was the case with my academics, it was something I seemed to excel at from an early age. Although the movements came naturally to me, I also worked extremely hard to perfect my gift. Initially, it was not for the sake of garnering critical acclaim or the recognition or approval of others, but rather for the love of my art. Like my classroom teachers, my ballet instructors saw my talent and my work ethic and were quick to single me out as the "can't-miss kid" (*e.g.,* "You have to go watch Courtney do this role, it's truly amazing" "Courtney's going all the way!"). In fact, when I was a 16-year-old sophomore in high school, I went to the School of American Ballet for an intensive summer program. I knew going in that after five weeks, the Ballet would ask a handful of girls to study at the prestigious school for the following school year. In the months leading up to the program, I'd told all of my friends and high school classmates that I'd absolutely love to be one of the chosen few. None of them expected me to be returning home for my junior year. In fact, I remember my high school friends and teachers tearfully wishing me goodbye. They just "knew" with the best of intentions, of course, that

I was going to make it big in New York. It didn't work out. To this day, I don't know if the tremendous pain I felt on hearing the news that I hadn't been selected was because I felt rejected or because I was terrified to go home and disappoint everyone by telling them I had not succeeded.

The following year, I went to the San Francisco Ballet School for the summer. I didn't really want the pressure, but I knew that if I wanted to pursue my dream, I had to find a way to push through it. I "redeemed" myself by being invited back the following summer, and ultimately achieved a coveted spot as a member of one of the world's most prestigious dance companies.

By then, however, I was caught in the same vicious cycle that had become the centerpiece of my academic life. I no longer was performing because I loved and longed to express myself through the art of my dance. I was performing to continually meet the extraordinarily high standards of those who believed in me, who sacrificed so much for me, who put their eye for artistic excellence on the line for me had come to expect of me—and I of myself. What none of those people realized, of course, was that the fear of not doing that, of not performing at my absolute best all the time made me sick to my stomach more times than I care to admit or think about. Not surprisingly, in the midst of the enormous pressure I put on myself, I lost sight of who I was as a dancer—independent of what the critics and the rest of the world was expecting—and the joy that once came with being able to freely express that part of me.

It all sort of came to a head two years ago during my eighth season as a professional dancer. In the course of that season, I broke numerous company records—for most ballets, most consecutive performances, many debuts in soloist roles, and opening night reviews in the local paper. I was exhausted and more than a little upset that I seemed to be receiving little to no recognition for all of my hard work. I knew in my heart that I was dancing at a soloist level and that I had earned the right to carry that title.

As it turned out, I didn't get the promotion I (and my peers) thought I deserved (I would have to wait another year for that), but, for the first time, I felt like I was successful even though perhaps in the eyes of others, I was not—and it was the greatest feeling of freedom I've ever known. For the first time in many years, I recognized my worth and talent and was comfortable with it, instead of constantly wondering if I was meeting others' expectations or approval and obsessing over whether my next performance would be as noteworthy as my previous one.

For me, that realization and the freedom that accompanied it came when I realized that I was blessed with the gift of dance—not so that I could be recognized (though, clearly the accolades are nice and appreciated), but rather so that I could "give it away" to those who came to see me perform.

That message was driven home to me recently when, sensing my anxiety before a role that I felt particularly unprepared to perform (I had only been given a week to learn it which left almost no time to focus on technique and artistry), an established principal dancer approached me and said: "Remember, Courtney, when you get out there, they can't touch you. You can worry all about what the staff and directors will think, but all of the artistic choices you make out there onstage, they're yours and yours alone. It's your moment alone with the audience, and it's about what you make them feel, not about whether or not this performance lives up to your last one." I say that to myself now all the time: 'They can't touch me up here. This is my time with the audience, and it's a privilege'."

Dear Ashley,

After much reflection, I have come to believe that author Marianne Williamson was right:

"[o]ur deepest fear is not that we are inadequate, but that we are powerful beyond measure …that it is our light, not our darkness that most frightens us. We ask ourselves: 'who are we to be brilliant, gorgeous, talented, fabulous,' when the question we should be asking is: who are we *not* to be? We are children of God. Our playing small does not serve the world. There is nothing enlightened about our shrinking so that other people won't feel insecure around us. We are all meant to shine, as children do. We were born to make manifest the glory of God that is within us. It's not just in some of us; it's in all of us. And as we let our own light shine, we unconsciously give other people permission to do the same. As we are liberated from our own fear of success, our presence automatically liberates others." [1]

My wish for both of us is that we will find the strength necessary to fully embrace this truth and the courage required to act on it.

With All My Love,
Dad

---

1   *A Return To Love: Reflections on the Principles of A Course in Miracles* by Marianne Williamson

CHAPTER 12

The First Step

(The fear of venturing out)

I've always been intrigued by the New Testament accounts of Peter's attempt to walk on water. It seems that one day, after preaching to the masses, Jesus sent the crowds away, instructed Peter and the other disciples to set out on their boats and went up on the mountain by himself to pray. As evening settled in, the disciples' boat, which already was some distance from the shore, was being battered and tossed about by waves stirred up by an approaching storm. Not surprisingly, the disciples became very fearful. Moments later, Jesus approached the boat, walking on the sea—a sight that, suffice it to say, only further terrified his followers. In fact, some cried out in a loud voice: "It's a ghost!" Eager to calm their fears, Jesus immediately spoke to them, saying, "Take courage, it is I; do not be afraid." Peter, as he was prone to do, stepped forward, and in what likely is the first recorded instance of "be careful what you ask for," boldly said to Him, "Lord, if it truly is You, command me to come to You on the water." Jesus responded: "Come!" According

75

to Matthew, Peter somehow mustered the courage to get out of the boat and began walking on the water toward Jesus. But, feeling the wind and the seas around him, Peter suddenly became frightened and began to sink. As he did, Peter cried out in desperation, "Lord, save me!" Jesus immediately stretched out His hand and took hold of Peter. Once He had him firmly in His grasp, Jesus said to him, "You of little faith, why did you doubt?" (Matthew 14: 22–33) Thereupon, they returned to the boat together, and upon their arrival, the wind stopped.

I often wonder what was really going through Peter's mind when in the midst of what by all Biblical accounts was a pretty severe storm, Jesus summoned him to leave the safety and security of his boat and walk across the water into his waiting arms. It's worth noting, of course, that this was not the first time that the courage and faith of Peter and the disciples had been put to the test. After all, shortly after their first meeting, Jesus invited them to leave behind everything to which they had grown accustomed—their family, their friends, their livelihoods, their possessions—and become "fishers of men," which they did. But walking on water in the midst of a storm?!? That was taking trust to a whole new level – a level, as the reader soon discovers, even Peter could only sustain for a fleeting moment, before the reality of what he had convinced himself to do (voluntarily step out of the boat and onto the raging seas) fully sank in and he with it!

Peter's dilemma in the midst of the storm is really no different from the dilemmas we encounter at various times in each of our life journeys. Do we stay where we are simply because it is safe, comfortable and predictable, even though we know that where we are is not everything it could, should or was intended to be? Or do we take a chance, venture out and embrace a new or different way of living and doing things? Do we stretch, take a risk, create opportunities for growth, recognizing that along the way, we are almost certain to encounter obstacles, be called upon to endure hardship and failures, and at times, be more than a little apprehensive, if not downright fearful?

Often, to the objective observer, the choice seems far more obvious than it is to the person confronted with it. Curiously, however, even those who are terribly afflicted with an eating disorder or other addictive behaviors often find some level of comfort and security in the status quo. Indeed, in ways that are well beyond my understanding, their identity becomes inextricably intertwined with their illness, so much so that they are reluctant to the point of aggression to give it up, even when presented with the prospect of a better, healthier life. Instead, they cling to the mantle of their illness and find comfort and security among those similarly afflicted and in the trappings that go along with being profoundly sick (*e.g.,* the regimented structure of in-patient life, attending one group therapy session after another, the medicine regimens, the camaraderie, etc.). Like Peter, they are reluctant to move away from the known, however dysfunctional and limiting it may appear to others, into the uncertainty of the unknown, or if they do test the waters, almost immediately long to jump back in the boat, even one that may be taking on water, and left unattended, almost certainly will sink!

I believe that the key to taking that critical first step is faith followed hastily by a serious amount of unconditional and sustained trust, as Peter so graphically illustrated in his first few steps. It is a reality that each of us experienced in our own lives, albeit at a time when we were much too young to grasp the full and complex import of the liberating moment, which, my prism tells me is why we are blessed with the chance to experience it time and time again:

Dear Ashley,

I doubt there are many challenges that you confronted as a 10-month-old child that were more difficult or more intimidating than the prospect of taking your first step. I suspect that, like most of us, you had grown pretty comfortable with life on all fours.

Sure it had its limitations. For one thing, your perspective on the world was limited to what was 10" off the ground, which undoubtedly made life a little scarier than it needed to be. It also meant that lots of things that probably looked pretty intriguing were out of your reach. Finally, even as quick as you had gotten at crawling (and you were pretty quick) it would never compare to the speed with which you could get from point A to point B if you could walk, let alone run!

But there was also a comfort level there that could not be overlooked. Most importantly, there was no risk of falling. You were firmly planted on the ground at all times, which meant that, aside from an occasional rug burn or an inadvertent shot to the side of the head by an inattentive foot, you were largely insulated from harm. You also knew that if you really needed to get from point A to point B faster or wanted something slightly out of your reach, you could simply make a face or pitch a fit and chances were someone would scoop "Your Cuteness" up and take you wherever you needed to go. Still, at some point, you decided that the benefits of walking outweighed the comforts of crawling, and so you began to entertain the idea of taking that first step.

I'll bet if Mom and I had been able to tap into your mind during those initial strategy sessions, we would have encountered the same range of thoughts and emotions that you have most recently been experiencing as you struggle with your eating disorder—apprehension, fear, uncertainty, curiosity, excitement, anticipation—just to name a few. And yet with all that stuff swimming around in your head, you set out on your journey.

You crawled over to a small table, and using all your strength, pulled yourself up to a standing (well, sort of standing?!?) position.

*Step 1 accomplished—a big smile that said: "I'm proud of me!"
Then came the first letting go, a bobble, a wobble, a look of sheer
terror, and back on the ground. Perhaps a tear or two because
it was supposed to hurt to fall, but then, an instant later, the
realization that the falling wasn't that bad after all. A moment
to regroup, then back to the table. Another pull-up—a step, a
bobble, a wobble, that same smile as you steadied yourself, and
then another step. A stumble, and then another fall, but this time
no tears—instead, a smile, twice as big as the first that said "I
got this!" An internal pat on the back—and then quickly back
to that table leg. This time you were up in a flash… you steadied
yourself, delivered a look of determination (by the way, I've since
seen that same exact look a time or two (thousand) in the past 19
years!), a step, no bobble, no wobble, and then another step, and
then another, and another. And before you knew it, you were in
Daddy's arms on the other side of the room, and the crowd (that
would be Mom and I) was going crazy!!!*

*You did it, and while, like all of us, you have mostly taken
it for granted, you have done it again and again and again
innumerable times since then. And you know what? Because
you've had lots of practice, you can do it again. I love you, Ashley,
for every step you have taken in your life since that first one, and
I encourage you to take the next one (and the one after that) with
confidence in you and the God who created you!*

With All My Love,
Dad

The Healing

CHAPTER 13

"Mr. Fix-It"

(Losing the control we never really had)

I (now) am the first to admit that, for as long as I can remember, I have been the quintessential example of what modern-day psychologists label as a Type A personality. Give me a task to do (actually, I would prefer that you give me 10 to do at the same time so that I may more clearly demonstrate my considerable skill at multi-tasking) and I almost certainly will overdo it. Present me with a new challenge, a new skill that needs acquiring, and I likely will devote whatever time and effort is required to master it. Better yet, tell me that you have a problem (or let me reach that conclusion on my own simply based on my perception of the "way things should be"—I'm very good at this unenviable skill) and, whether you ask for my help or not, I will invariably set about trying to find a solution for you – in most cases more than one, just in case you don't like the first one, or God forbid, it doesn't play out precisely the way I had hoped that it would.

The truth is that from the time I was a very young man, I have always thrived on solving other people's problems. It was something

I seemed to be good at—a gift, if you will—and friends and family members often sought me out for help. Over time, I also excelled (or so I thought) at anticipating problems before they arose, and through careful planning (some might fairly refer to it as unhealthy micro-management), I managed to head them off at the pass before they fully materialized. In the case of my children, I rationalized my behavior by convincing myself that all I was really doing was my best to insulate them from the pain, disappointment, anxiety, heartache and frustration that often arises when things don't go precisely as we had hoped or planned. I suppose, in this respect, I was no different from many parents who long to shield their children from even the slightest physical, emotional or psychological harm, and in the process, try to preserve the innocence of childhood as long as possible. Somewhere along the way, however, my "Mr. Fix-It" mentality morphed into a misguided belief that I could actually control events and experiences that are an inevitable and necessary part of all of our lives, including the lives of our children.

And then, one day, my daughter stopped eating…

As long as I live (and as hard as I've tried), I will never forget that February morning when I first walked through the door of the small two-bedroom apartment that I had rented for my wife and daughter shortly after we learned she was sick, less than a stone's throw from the gates leading to the University of Southern California. Despite the fact that it was unseasonably warm outside and the air conditioning in the unit was turned off, there, in a nearly fetal position, wrapped in a woolen blanket in the corner of the oversized couch that dominated the small living room, was a frail and frightened young woman who I barely recognized as my daughter.

Her eyes, which just a few months earlier radiated with the joy, excitement and anticipation of life as a college freshman, bore the unmistakable look of desperation, fear and hopelessness. They were bloodshot and swollen from tears, sunken in sockets disturbingly prominent among the rest of the pale, drawn features in her face. As I glanced down, I saw her hands, bony imposters of their tender predecessors, clinging to a small 8-ounce aluminum can of Ensure®, a high-protein drink I had only recently heard of, an apparent staple of those unable (or unwilling) to eat "normal" food. Out of its tiny lid emerged a straw, only inches from her parched and quivering lips which were desperate for even a brief reminder of what food or liquid tasted like. I hardly knew what to say, let alone do. It all seemed so surrealistic, so incredibly irrational.

And so there the three of us sat (my wife, daughter and I) armed with the knowledge that if Ashley didn't eat or drink something soon, she was likely going to die, and at the same time confronted by the harsh realization that she and her eating disorder, which by then was firmly in control of the situation, couldn't possibly care any less. Indeed, both were openly, almost combatively, defiant. Miraculously, after two-and-a-half hours of encouraging, cajoling, tearfully imploring, insisting and ultimately dictating in anger, the task was complete—the small can empty—just in time to start the gut-wrenching process all over again. Already I'd seen enough.

I responded, much like Pavlov's dog, by immediately leaping into action. I threw my entire arsenal of problem-solving skills at her eating disorder. I began by researching and identifying all of the leading experts in the field and then spoke to them, one by one, in search of understanding. I used what I was able to learn to try and put together a game plan—a course of treatment that most certainly would dispel this insidious enemy just as quickly as "he" had moved in and taken hostage the most beautiful soul I have ever known.

Ultimately, however, I came to a very sobering and heartbreaking realization: there I was, confronted with the biggest and most important problem I had ever faced, with my daughter's life, a life for which I would gladly and unhesitatingly sacrifice my own, literally hanging in the balance, and I was powerless to fix it. In fact, truth be told, I couldn't even understand it.

Over time, years in fact, I have come to embrace a far more liberating truth: If we are to take to heart the assurance that we are created in the image and likeness of God, it seems highly unlikely that there is really much for us to fix. Indeed, the more likely reality is that, in our efforts to fix things or, worse yet, fix each other, we are almost certain to do more harm than good. Instead, my sense is that our role, as individuals and as parents, is to embrace and fully rejoice in the gift and uniqueness that is every aspect of our and our children's creation, to respect and nurture those creations with unconditional love and support, and, in the process, to learn to accept the reality that there are many things about ourselves and about others, including our children, that we simply cannot and never were intended to control, let alone fix, even things that may subject them and us to profound challenges and suffering.

Dear Ashley,

It's been nearly two months since I've written a word. Something happened between you and me several weeks ago that knocked me off my mark and took me by complete surprise. You said things to me (actually, you screamed them at me) that you had never said to me before, things that were hurtful, things that, candidly, I thought were unjustified, and in large measure, historically incorrect. The following day (and for several days thereafter), you were very apologetic and remorseful. You told me you didn't mean what you said, that none of it was true. In fact, you claimed not to remember much of what you said. Ultimately, I forgave you, in part, because I know that your words didn't emanate from the heart that I've known and loved for the past 22 years, but rather from a hurt-filled place, and, in part, because I can't help but think that, as much as I may never have intended to do so, either by my words or my actions, I contributed to that hurt—or at least you feel that I did, which is a realization that is terribly hard for me to accept or know what to do with.

Still, on some level, I'm glad I took a break. It allowed me to take a step back and question my motives in writing this book and whether I have any business writing it at all. Most importantly, it reminded me of the power of words and the corresponding need to choose them very carefully. It also made me emotionally available to see something during my walk tonight that will be forever transfixed in my mind—something that I'm sure I've seen a thousand times before, but which never struck me quite the way it did tonight.

It was a young mother standing in a loud and congested parking lot, tenderly holding her nearly newborn infant close against her chest. That was it! "It" was the purest, most simplistic, most powerful and most beautiful expression of unconditional love I think I may have ever seen. "It" didn't require any words; in fact, mom was incapable of communicating with daughter at all, save for the delicate way she was cradling her and her willingness to allow her chest to serve as a pillow for a moment's rest. And yet, there is no doubt in my mind that as their hearts beat together, mom and infant child were fully engaged in unconditionally loving and accepting love from each other. I smiled as I walked by—and "mom" couldn't help but smile back.

As I passed by a second time, I thought about stopping to share with her how overwhelmed I was by the sight of her and her child, but our social mores really don't allow for intrusions like that by a stranger, nor did I want to intrude on the moment. If I could have mustered the courage, however, I would have urged her to dedicate her life to preserving and trying to duplicate that moment, not only with her child, but with everyone she held dear.

Instead, I continued on my way and I remembered holding you like that. I remembered how very special that felt. I remembered wondering how it was possible to love someone you barely even knew so completely. I remembered feeling overwhelmed by a sense of responsibility to provide for you, to protect you and to guide you. And yet, in the end, unbeknownst to me at the time, what I was most responsible for was "simply" preserving and finding new ways to communicate that same sense of unconditional love that we shared in our own parking lots innumerable times, when you couldn't say a word or understand a word I said. At one time or another, all of us have experienced the love that I saw in that parking lot tonight. Our challenge is to find our way back to it and then get out of our own way and allow it to take up residence in our soul. I want you to know that I intend to do that in my own life, and I encourage you to do the same.

With All My Love,
Dad

CHAPTER 14

The Girl on the Park Bench

(The freedom that comes from realizing
that we may not have all the answers)

I'm not sure what it is about the human condition that convinces us that we have or should have all of the answers to all of life's questions and challenges. Even more disturbingly, many of us actually come to believe it is a sign of weakness or inadequacy to reach out to others for help—no matter how desperate our circumstances and the corresponding need for assistance may be. In short, we would rather appear to be strong and in control than be perceived as weak and needy, even if it means continuing to suffer or struggle due to our inevitable inability to do it all on our own. I suspect that pride and ego play an important part in erecting these often impenetrable barriers that exist between our need for help and our willingness to embrace it. A reluctance to trust also likely plays a part in our determination to be self-reliant. Regardless of the cause, however, the results are the same: unhealthy stubbornness and isolation.

During the course of our daughter's illness, my wife and I participated in a group exercise designed to illustrate the fact that, at various times in our lives, all of us stand to benefit greatly from trusting others' insights and vision in times of need. The moderator of the group created an intricate maze of obstacles using objects of various shapes and sizes, some of which were very tenuously stacked on top of one another. He created the maze inside a large square on the floor whose perimeter was marked by 4"-in-diameter foam tubes. The group was then divided into two teams, each of which was required to select one of its members to enter the maze BLINDFOLDED! They, in turn, would receive verbal instruction from their sighted teammates in how to negotiate the maze. The first team to get all of its members, one at a time, to the other side of the maze without knocking over a single obstacle would be declared the winner.

Our team selected my daughter, perhaps one of the most stubborn, hell-bent on being self-reliant people on the planet (aside from her dad?!?) to be our first blindfolded participant. I can only imagine the immediate sense of discomfort she felt the minute she realized that this was something she couldn't possibly do on her own. In fact, she couldn't even make it over the tubing that outlined the maze's perimeter without the aid of her teammates—all of whom had a singular purpose: getting her to the other side of the maze unblemished. I will never forget the surprising sense of responsibility I felt as the person chosen by the team to guide her through that obstacle course, one painstaking step (or, on some occasions, a half-step) at a time. After all, it was just a simple exercise, and it wasn't as if anyone's feelings or health hung in the balance. I also will never forget the sense of relief and accomplishment both of us felt (as well as the smile on her face) when, some 15 minutes later, she safely stepped across the perimeter on the other side of the 20-foot span, having made it through the course without so much as brushing against, let alone knocking over, any of the obstacles.

Dear Ashley,

    Another walk in the park, another revelation …

    As I was crossing the bridge that leads from the parking lot to the jogging trail, I saw a beautiful young woman, who I believe was between 15 and 17 years old, sitting on a park bench with what appeared to be a third-grade reader in her hand. At her side was an older woman, a tutor, who, I suspect, was a complete stranger to the young lady until she decided that she needed to learn how to read if she was ever going to fully experience and enjoy all that life has to offer.

    Later, as I passed in front of the bench, I heard the young woman struggle and then stumble over a few words, which, it occurred to me, you probably understood and could clearly pronounce when you were little more than six years old (Note: I'm not bragging here; I'm just stating facts to make a point). She was clearly frustrated and more than a little bit embarrassed. I, on the other hand, was deeply moved by the simplicity and wisdom of the tutor's response – "It's o.k. Try again."

    The tutor knew that while the words on that page were simple to most, they seemed like an insurmountable obstacle to someone who had never learned to read, likely in the same way conquering this insidious illness seems to you at this moment. She also knew, however, that by making the decision to learn how to read and by reaching out to someone who could teach her, the young woman already had won the battle. The rest of the fight and her ultimate victory over illiteracy were only a matter of time.

    Ashley, you are no different from that beautiful young woman. You are fighting a battle against an enemy that you don't fully understand and have never been taught to do battle with before. Commit to winning the fight and reach out to those who have helped hundreds of others learn the skills required to conquer this despicable foe. Don't be afraid to find your own teachers and then to surrender and humble yourself before them. And when you stumble, as you most certainly will along the way, remember—"It's o.k. Try again."

With All My Love,
Dad

CHAPTER 15

The Miners

(Contrary to popular belief, hope is not a light that awaits our arrival at the end of the proverbial tunnel)

On October 13, 2010, much of the civilized world (at least those with access to a T.V. set or computer) held its collective breath as a high-tech capsule was lowered into the San José copper/gold mine in the Atacama Desert near Copiapó, Chile. It was the beginning of the final chapter in what had been a dramatic (if not historic) effort to rescue 33 men who had been trapped 2,300 feet below the surface of the Earth for more than 69 days. For most, the rescue effort represented the triumph of human ingenuity and technology. It was, after all, technology and engineering (a small bore hole the size of a grapefruit) that first allowed rescuers to locate signs of life buried under nearly ½ a mile of rock and debris 17 days after the mine collapsed, when most had long since given the miners up for dead. Technology also was what enabled those same rescuers to use that narrow shaft, known as a "paloma" (the Spanish word for dove), to ensure that the miners received the essentials of life (*i.e.*, water, food, etc.) and later, as a vital means of communicating with relatives, loved ones and other supporters on the surface, through letters and, ultimately, via video messages. Finally, technology and the minds of more than two dozen NASA and Chilean engineers and medical experts were what enabled rescuers to devise and implement a highly sophisticated plan that would eventually lead to the successful rescue effort—a plan that included drilling and reinforcing the walls of a second shaft the width of a bicycle tire and then designing what turned out to be a 13-foot-long pod weighing nearly 1,000 pounds. The pod, appropriately nicknamed "Phoenix" after the mythical creature that rose from the ashes, was capable of accommodating one miner at a time for what the experts anticipated would be a 15-minute, round-trip journey to the surface.

For me, however, the Chilean mine disaster and the elaborate rescue efforts that followed represented far more than just another, albeit unusually public, display of the human mind at work. After all, by definition, rescue efforts depend on there being someone to rescue—in this case 33 men who set out for work on August 5, as they had done countless times in the past, wholly unaware of the life-threatening events with which they would be confronted before day's end. Days after the rescue, glimpses of the mine collapse and the terrifying moments and days that followed began to emerge from interviews with the rescued miners. We know, for example, that an impenetrable darkness engulfed the miners as more than 700,000 tons of rock descended on the mine shaft. We know that, at best, each of the men had the benefit of only a 48- to 96-hour emergency supply of food and an even shorter supply of potable water. We also know that the temperatures in the mine following the collapse hovered around 100°F and that the breathable air in the small 500 sq. ft. space that the men occupied, left unreplenished, would not sustain life indefinitely. And yet, in spite of all of this, we know that, within 24 hours of the collapse, these men, virtual strangers to one another, from wildly disparate backgrounds, who ranged in age from 19 to 64 and in mining experience from veritable novices (*i.e.*, 5 days in the mine) to those with more than 52 years of service, began working together as a team fixated on a common goal—survival. That they did so, under such extreme stress and with no reasonable basis for believing they would ever get out of the mine alive, is almost inexplicable save for the fact that for all of their dissimilarities, the men had one gift in common—each harbored a seed of hope.

I suspect that when the rest of the story is told, we will learn that in the initial hours and days following the collapse, some of those 33 men leapt to the forefront and immediately began to manage the crisis; their seed of hope had been germinated long before they ever set foot in the mine that August morning, either through life circumstances that demanded or benefited from its active presence or simply as a by-product of their unwavering faith in God. In others, the seed, though dormant due to their youth, lack of life experience or simply good fortune, likely required only a minimal amount of prodding and encouragement to spring forth into life and begin to take root. Still others almost certainly had long since buried their seeds beneath layers and layers of disappointment, heartache, frustration, rejection, loneliness, and unfulfilled or shattered dreams. If they had faith, it had long since been displaced by fear or a sense of abandonment. For them, the journey to re-discovering and embracing what was left of their fragile seeds of hope would be a long and difficult one marred by setbacks—a virtual tug-of-war waged between their heart's fundamental desire to join their fellow miners in believing that a new and brighter tomorrow was waiting just over the horizon and their mind's eye, whose once-clear view of that horizon had been obscured by what it perceived to be the seemingly never-ending, painful realities of everyday life.

And so it is with each of us. At some point in our lives, we will encounter the darkness that invariably accompanies a sense that the walls are caving in around us—albeit in a much less literal and dramatic way than they did that August morning around our Chilean brothers. The source of the darkness will take many forms, and its intensity and duration will vary greatly from one person to the next. For some, the darkness will emanate from rejection, abandonment, a trust breached, a love or friendship lost. For others, the darkness will be tied to physical, emotional or psychological illness, the death of a loved one, the loss of a job, a feeling of extreme inadequacy or a traumatic event. More often than not, the darkness will be temporary, like a morning fog, momentarily engulfing everything in its reach only to burn off hours, days or even weeks later and reveal the magnificence of the landscape beneath. On occasion, however, the darkness will seem impenetrable, all-consuming, suffocating. When it does, panic will set in, as it almost certainly did in the hearts and minds of those trapped in the San José mine moments after its walls collapsed. With that panic will come a sense of desperation and helplessness.

I know, because I've been in that dark place many times over the past several years. Even more disturbingly and heartbreakingly, I've seen that sense of hopelessness in my daughter's eyes and heard it in her words, as I have in the eyes and words of countless young women in the death grip of an eating disorder, more times than I care to think about.

Like them and countless others, I have flailed about in the darkness, searching for someone or something to serve as a light at the end of what often seemed like an endless tunnel. Largely as a result of the reflections and revelations in this book, however, I ultimately came to a critical and liberating realization: hope is not a light that waits impatiently for our arrival at the end of that proverbial tunnel. Rather, it is the light within each of us, which, when patiently and properly nurtured, helps to illuminate and penetrate the darkness inside the tunnel so that we can navigate our own way out—one sometimes joyful, often painstaking, but always purposeful step after another.

Dear Ashley,

I was thinking of you today and this very early, but spectacularly beautiful and tender work of Emily Dickinson came to mind:

Hope is the Thing with Feathers
"Hope" is the thing with feathers
That perches in the soul
And sings the tune without the words
And never stops at all,

And sweetest in the gale is heard;
And sore must be the storm
That could abash the little bird
That kept so many warm.

I've heard it in the chillest land
And on the strangest sea,
Yet never, in extremity,
It asked a crumb of me.

My prayer is that, in those moments when the noise of the surrounding storm subsides, you will hear the chirping in your soul and take heart. You are loved—beyond words.

With All My Love,

Dad

CHAPTER 16

The Monarch

("Just when the caterpillar thought its
life was over"—A case study in patience)

The Monarch butterfly is one of God's most intrinsically beautiful and delicate creatures. I'm reasonably certain I was first introduced to the Monarch no later than the third grade. What I am considerably less sure about is why it took me nearly 45 years, a refrigerator magnet and my daughter's life-threatening illness to really get to know the Monarch's story, and more importantly, to begin to acquire what to the Monarch is an instinctive character trait that is essential to its and our own growth and survival: patience.

I'm probably the last person on earth who has any business writing about patience. In fact, prior to my daughter's illness, if you were to ask anyone who knew me for more than two hours or who had the misfortune to accompany me out to dinner at a crowded restaurant to describe my personality using five adjectives or less, one of the first almost assuredly would have been "impatient." The truth is, from the time I was a young boy, I hated to wait for anyone or anything—for any reason. It's not a trait I was particularly proud of, nor was it one that likely added to my life expectancy. It also did little to endear me to my children, my wife or my co-workers. To the contrary, my insistence that things get done "yesterday" was a constant source of considerable stress to everyone within my sphere of influence.

I can't really pinpoint where my almost pathologic sense of impatience originated or why it became such a prominent feature in my life. After all, I grew up prior to the advent of many of the technological advances that served to fuel the "there-has-to-be-a-way-I-can-get-this-done-faster" mentality that became the cornerstone of my children's generation, and in the process, turned impatience into a veritable art form. I'm thinking particularly of simple things that we now take for granted, but that were only a figment of someone's imagination when I was growing up (*e.g.*, microwave ovens, cell phones, fax machines, DVRs and DVDs, Blackberrys, personal computers, the Internet, Twitter, social networking sites and eBay)—not to mention advances in science, medications and medical procedures that have dramatically improved the diagnosis and treatment of a variety of ailments.

During my childhood and young adulthood, I actually had to wait more than 1½ minutes for a meal to cook and until the next day at school to find out what transpired between the final bell of the preceding day and the morning bell of the next in the lives of each of my friends. I had to catch movies while they were still in the theater if I wanted to see them, to wait for a favorite song to find its way onto the shelves at the local record store to hear it, and longer still to acquire many of the sporting goods and other objects I coveted—a by-product, in part, of my family's modest financial resources and a mom and dad who grew up in relatively poor families with a clear appreciation for the value of a dollar. Nothing in my world happened very fast, let alone as fast as I would have liked—a fact that never seemed to bother most of my peers, but drove me crazy. I'm not sure whether, paradoxically, the turtle-like aspects of my circumstances gave birth to my impatience or simply fed a personality trait that was there from the beginning, but I do know I grew to be VERY IMPATIENT.

I also know that, on some level, both by the example of impatience I exhibited in my daily interactions with others and the speed with which I responded to familial needs and wants, I passed this unfortunate character trait onto both of my children. The practical ramifications of that in a consumption-based society are obvious. What is less apparent, but of much greater consequence, however, is the way that impatience plays out in our daily lives as individuals and as parents. At some point, we no longer simply desire things to happen more rapidly, we expect them to, and we become frustrated, disappointed, and angry when events and others don't cooperate with our expectations and timetables. Regrettably, that is true in all aspects of our lives—our growing up, our relationships, our educational journeys, our advancement at work, our parenting, even, in the case of illness, our willingness to allow for meaningful and lasting healing to occur.

Both my daughter and I brought our collective impatience to her illness and, candidly, it was nearly the end of both of us—me in a figurative way and her in a much more literal one. And then one day, in the darkest hours of my daughter's struggles, I focused for the first time on a simple magnet that she had placed on the door of our refrigerator—a magnet with a message which I'm certain I'd seen on at least a hundred prior trips to the refrigerator. The magnet had been a gift from a very compassionate life coach who we were fortunate to meet early on in Ashley's battle. It depicted a strikingly beautiful Monarch butterfly effortlessly gliding over the following inscription: "Just when the caterpillar thought the world was over, she became a butterfly!" It was precisely the message I needed to hear at that moment in my life—and one that spoke to my heart. I hurried to my laptop to learn as much as I could about this magical creature. In the process, I discovered some fascinating parallels between the Monarch's life journey and our own, and a critical life lesson.

The life of a Monarch butterfly begins innocently enough as eggs laid on milkweed plants. Usually after 4 or 5 days, the eggs hatch into baby caterpillars which are also known as larvae. For the next two weeks, the baby caterpillars do little more than eat the milkweed plants! It's hardly what most humans would consider a terribly inspiring, let alone glamorous existence, particularly given that, unbeknownst to the caterpillar at the time, the larvae stage will consume approximately 30% of what will be the Monarch's entire lifetime. In human terms, that would be the equivalent of our sitting at the kitchen table for nearly 30 years of non-stop eating! As it turns out, however, as routine and tedious as it may seem, the time and patience that the unsuspecting caterpillar devotes to eating the milkweed is an indispensable first step in acquiring the strength required to continue and ultimately complete the next and perhaps most unique step in its magical life journey.

After two weeks of non-stop eating, the fully grown caterpillar manufactures tiny silk fibers to attach itself to a leaf or a stem on the milkweed plant. Within hours, its new skin hardens to form what to the outside world appears to be a rather unsightly, if not downright ugly, misshapen pod known as a chrysalis. It is within the safety and security of the chrysalis that the caterpillar undergoes the mysterious, life-changing process known as metamorphosis—a remarkable period during which the caterpillar's old body parts are transformed into those needed to give birth to the Monarch. The process, which one senses must seem incredibly confusing and traumatic to the caterpillar, takes approximately 10 days—fully 25% of the Monarch's total lifespan. But it is hardly the end of its journey.

In fact, as the adult insect emerges from the chrysalis, upside down, it is in its most delicate and vulnerable state. Its abdomen is filled with fluid and its wings are wet and crumpled, incapable of sustaining flight. Consequently, at a time when it is likely most restless, the Monarch instinctively knows that its life depends on its ability to remain very still for another few hours, while the fluid in its abdomen is pumped into the veins of its tiny wings. Were it to do otherwise (*i.e.*, were the Monarch to attempt to fly before the fluid transfer is complete), its wings would dry crumpled—leaving the Monarch helpless to escape waiting predators or find the food it needs to flourish. And so it does what is required: it remains still for just a few more hours, and its patience is richly rewarded—with the ability to fly in splendor for the remainder of its life.

Dear Ashley,

When I was growing up, I wanted to rush everything about life. I remember counting the days until I could get my driver's license, convinced that the freedom it afforded would change my life; and yet, when the time finally came, it occurred to me that 16 years old was awfully young to be navigating the highways of South Florida. The truth is: I was scared to death, and in retrospect, thought I would have been much better off and likely not missed out on a whole lot had I waited a little longer, until I was a little more responsible, a little more mature, before getting behind the wheel.

I was equally impatient where school was concerned. I couldn't wait to go to high school and then to college (or so I thought). I had fantasized about what it would be like to finally be away from home, away from my parents' supervision, answerable only to myself, free to do whatever I pleased whenever I pleased, and in my mind, that day couldn't possibly come soon enough; and then it came and, as my parents pulled away from the dorm for the last time, I was scared to death. Left alone in a sea of strangers, it occurred to me, in retrospect, that 17 years old was awfully young to be left to my own devices, especially when I was so insecure and my "devices" were so grossly underdeveloped.

Still, my impatience, dwarfed only by my stubbornness, persisted. Next on my radar screen was marriage. I was 22 years old. I had no real idea who I was as a person and no viable means of supporting myself, let alone someone else. But I convinced myself I was ready and that starting a life together couldn't happen fast enough; and then it did and, again, I was in way over my head. It occurred to me, in retrospect, that 22 years old was awfully young to be making a lifetime commitment and that neither we, nor our relationship would have been disserved by waiting just a few more years—at least until I'd graduated from law school and settled down.

You reminded me a lot of myself when you were young. You shared my impatience. You set your sights on a target and then charted a course designed to achieve that goal as quickly and efficiently as humanly possible—in some instances, even quicker than seemed humanly possible. It was important for you to be first to the finish line—and more often than not you were. I likely even encouraged and applauded your efforts, never fully realizing the heavy price that both of us ultimately would pay for our hurriedness, our impatience.

And then you and I learned about your illness and realized the hard way that no amount of impatience on your part or mine was going to accelerate the healing process. To the contrary, it quickly became clear to me that your healing (our healing) demanded patience, and so I began to learn what patience looked and felt like. I've still got an awful lot left to learn, but so far, I like what I see. Like most change, it's not an easy process. Fortunately for you, you have a 30-year head start on me! So, take your time and embrace what the Monarch has to teach us: that in life, it's the fullness with which you reach the finish line, not how quickly you get there that ultimately matters most.

With All My Love,

Dad

CHAPTER 17

A Young Mother and Her Two Little Boys

(And other everyday acts of courage)

I suspect if you were to ask 100 people on the street to define and give an example of courage, 90 percent of them would respond in a fairly predictable manner—and justifiably so. That's because most of us were raised with a Merriam-Webster-like definition of courage—one that contemplates a sense of fearlessness on the part of its possessor, one that is dependent for its expression on another being in harm's way and in need of either protection or rescue, one that suggests that courage is a unique virtue possessed by a relatively few chosen individuals, and, finally, one that equates courage with bravery.

Consequently, their examples of courage would likely be equally predictable. Some would point to the unforgettable images of 9/11 and the countless first responders, who, knowing full well that they likely would be sacrificing their lives in the process, poured into the Twin

Towers in the hope that they could rescue or at a minimum, comfort the thousands of innocent victims trapped inside. Others likely would relate stories of military personnel, perhaps even family members or friends, who, often against seemingly insurmountable odds and in the face of almost certain death, selflessly sacrificed their own life in an effort to save the lives of a fellow soldier or a civilian. Still others might recount instances where a bystander happened upon the scene of a horrific accident, a crime, a house fire, a flash flood or a submerged vehicle and, seemingly without hesitation, put their personal safety aside to shield or remove another human being from harm. Needless to say, each of these is a valid and admirable example of a courageous individual and act.

My journey, however, has led me to embrace a slightly different, more expansive definition of courage, one that plainly is broad enough to encompass the more traditional acts that all of us rightfully associate with the word, while at the same time recognizing as equally courageous the often more subtle, sometimes almost imperceptible, and always far less public choices that many, including those afflicted with eating disorders and other addictive behaviors and emotional illnesses, make, not for the sake of saving someone else's life, but in deciding to live another day, and in the process, save their own. I found that definition, oddly enough, in the words of beatnik writer, James Neil Hollingworth (1933–1996), who, writing under the pen name Ambrose Redmoon, once described courage "[not as] the absence of fear, but rather [as a] judgment that something else is more important than fear."

Looking through my newfound prism, I have since caught glimpses of those acts of courage played out in the lives of countless young and not-so-young women in eating disorder treatment facilities across the country. I have heard it in the halting words of an exceptionally beautiful 18-year-old-girl, who, having first simultaneously disclosed to her parents and a group of relative strangers that she had been raped by someone she thought was a friend on what was supposed to be a casual night out, struggled to take the first steps toward trusting others as well as her own judgment again. I also have seen it in the frightened face of a young mother of two little boys, who confronted the fear and heartache of leaving them behind to seek the treatment she desperately needed, despite the insensitive, indeed abusive threats of her husband that if she acted on what he deemed to be the selfish course of conduct she was considering, he would leave her and the kids—knowing that, at the end of the day, her physical and emotional well-being might be the only hope those little boys had. On a much more simplistic level, I have seen it standing in a food line amidst a group of girls, who, terrified by the distorted images of self that reflected back at them in the morning mirror, found the strength to choose from a cafeteria-style selection of food items, and with the support of friends, fight through three substantial meals and two snacks a day for months at a time on a sometimes insanely difficult and always incremental road to recovery.

And I have seen it in the life of my own daughter, both before and during her illness. In fact, as I look back, it was courage which at the age of 5, caused Ashley to stand on principle, even if at the time the "principle" was that she should not be forced to wear a silly-looking Russian fur hat over a hair bun that she and her mom had spent hours carefully crafting, and the "standing" part was quite literally done, hands folded with a scowl on her face, at center stage during a dance recital, in an auditorium filled with hundreds of parents, teachers and school administrators! Her Redmoon-esque courage also was on full display in the speed and eagerness with which she remounted and rode a horse that only several months earlier was at least partially responsible, albeit not in an intentional way, in her severely breaking her hip and having to spend the better part of her 14th summer wheelchair-bound and in a body cast that only the Marquis de Sade could have contrived. It was a fall that very easily could have killed her, if not relegated her to that wheelchair for the rest of her life.

Later on, it would be that same courage that, standing at death's doorstep, would allow Ashley's caretakers to insert a feeding tube in her nose, knowing that it would be there for weeks, if not months, providing her with nutrition—at a time when every aspect of her being rebelled against the idea of being fed. Indeed, as I look back on it now, with considerably more perspective than I had at the time, that courage was evident from the day I first encountered her in the throes of her disease, as she mustered the strength to bring the straw sticking out of that bottle of Ensure to her lips—time and time again—hour after excruciating hour. And, ultimately, it is courage that enables her and others in recovery to greet the many challenges that they still face each day in search of a brighter, less conflicted, healthier tomorrow (*e.g.,* issues relating to body image, shame, feelings of inadequacy, unworthiness, trust, control, etc.) and still keep going.

These experiences have led me to conclude that it is critically important for parents, siblings, extended family members, teachers, school administrators, ministers, colleagues, classmates, coaches, counselors, treating physicians and, in some instances, even complete strangers to be able to recognize and appropriately acknowledge manifestations of courage in all its forms, large and small, whether they occur on the battlefield or on the playing field, in the classroom or in the boardroom, in public or, in the case of a disordered eater, hunched over a toilet seat with a split second decision to make, in the privacy of a bathroom. I also have come to believe, contrary to what many social commentators and critics have suggested over the years, that doing so will not serve to trivialize or dilute the significance of the uniquely "brave" events that we historically have singled out for such accolades. Instead, it will ensure that those who are equally courageous, albeit often in a far less public and spectacular fashion, will become more fully aware of their capacity to confront and overcome fear, and in the process, create a space and an opportunity for the seed of hope to take root and flourish.

Dear Ashley,

Two days ago, I came across the following quote:

"Courage is not the absence of fear; it is the judgment that there are things that are more important than fear," and I wondered if I have ever really shared with you just how COURAGEOUS you are and just how much I admire that quality in you.

The truth is that you have been putting fear in its proper place all your life:

You fought your way into this world (quite prematurely—I might add!) when doctors said you wouldn't make it. You endured 3 surgeries before you were even 4 years old.

You badly fractured your hip and 6 months later competed at the Region 12 Arabian Hunter Jumper Championships.

You once were afraid of being on stage, but later performed before tens of thousands of people all over the world, and in the process, brought immeasurable joy into their lives.

I encourage you to once again overcome whatever fears now confront you.

EACH MORNING FOR THE NEXT 25 DAYS PUT A ☺ IN THE SPACE NEXT TO THE OBJECT THAT IS "MORE IMPORTANT" TO YOU AND THEN WORK HARD TO LIVE THE DAY COURAGEOUSLY:

____	MY LIFE	____	Self-Destructive Behaviors
____	MY RELATIONSHIP WITH FAMILY	____	Self-Destructive Behaviors
____	MY FAITH	____	Self-Destructive Behaviors
____	MY RELATIONSHIP WITH FRIENDS	____	Self-Destructive Behaviors
____	MY HEART	____	Self-Destructive Behaviors
____	MY MIND	____	Self-Destructive Behaviors
____	MY CREATIVITY	____	Self-Destructive Behaviors
____	MUSIC	____	Self-Destructive Behaviors
____	STUDYING OR LIVING OVERSEAS	____	Self-Destructive Behaviors
____	HORSEBACK RIDING	____	Self-Destructive Behaviors
____	WRITING	____	Self-Destructive Behaviors
____	PURSUING MY DREAMS	____	Self-Destructive Behaviors
____	MY GIFTS AND INNER BEAUTY	____	Self-Destructive Behaviors
____	HAVING A POSITIVE INFLUENCE ON OTHERS' LIVES	____	Self-Destructive Behaviors
____	A GOOD NIGHT'S SLEEP	____	Self-Destructive Behaviors
____	DRIVING JIMI (ANYWHERE)	____	Self-Destructive Behaviors
____	SITTING ON A BEACH AT SUNSET	____	Self-Destructive Behaviors
____	WATCHING A GREAT FILM (or 3)	____	Self-Destructive Behaviors
____	ENJOYING A COLLEGE FOOTBALL GAME ON A COOL FALL AFTERNOON	____	Self-Destructive Behaviors

_____ BEING THERE FOR A   _____ Self-Destructive Behaviors
      FRIEND
_____ SHARING STARBUCKS   _____ Self-Destructive Behaviors
      WITH A FRIEND (OR MY
      DAD)
_____ STOPPING BY A CHURCH   _____ Self-Destructive Behaviors
      TO THANK GOD
      FOR GIVING ME THE
      COURAGE TO PUT A ☺
      BESIDE EACH ITEM IN
      THE LEFT-HAND COLUMN

ALL OF US (YOUR FAMILY, YOUR FRIENDS, and YOUR DOCTORS) LOVE YOU AND BELIEVE IN YOU.

With All My Love,

Dad

CHAPTER 18

Derek and Jim

(Finding joy and wonder in the uncertainty of the journey)

I often wonder how different our lives would be if the obnoxious blare of the morning alarm clock, the piercing sound that penetrates our brains with the reminder that it's time to "get up and do it all again," was replaced by the gentle tap of a messenger from God unequivocally promising us that before the day is over, whatever we wish for most that day will be ours. Imagine, for example: (1) a ballerina coming off a restless night's sleep in anticipation of an opening night performance that will mark her first appearance on stage as a member of one of the world's premier dance companies being assured by her "guardian angel" that, the following morning, critics' columns around the country will be echoing each others' praises for her exceptional talents and performance; (2) a lawyer poised to give final argument in the most important case of his life being promised that when the time comes for the jury to render its verdict, he will have convinced them to award the largest judgment ever handed down in a case of its type in the history of the state's jurisprudence;

(3) an actress scheduled to audition with hundreds of other equally talented and hungry colleagues for the starring role in an upcoming major motion picture being told that the director and casting agent will be so impressed with her performance that, before she can even reach the elevator to go home and await a callback, she will be told she got the part; (4) a professional athlete about to take the field in the most important game, round, race, or match of her life, knowing that when the final bell sounds, the last stroke is played, the final lap is run or swum, or the last point is won, she not only will have prevailed against her opponents, but she will have done so in record-breaking fashion; (5) a lover, uncertain of the future of her relationship, being told that, before she climbs back into bed, her hand will have been enthusiastically sought in marriage; (6) a young boy, whose gentle spirit has been ravaged by the unrelenting abuse of elementary or high school bullies, being assured of a day of peace and the warm embrace of a new friend; or (7) perhaps even more dramatically, one suffering from chronic, if not terminal illness, fearful of a mid-afternoon visit to the doctor to learn the results of the latest CAT scan, receiving a covenant that, much to his and his doctors' astonishment, his illness will have mysteriously, miraculously disappeared.

You don't have to be clairvoyant to imagine the immediate impact such a divine wake-up call likely would have in each of our lives. Among other things, there would be no further need for a snooze button—that clever device created, I suspect, to postpone the inevitable need to get up for an extra 10 or 15 minutes, in the hope that in the meantime, news would break of blizzard-like conditions or the imminent arrival of a hurricane, which, in turn, would enable us to spend the rest of the day in bed!

No, in the world I'm envisioning, every day would be like Christmas morning is to those still young enough to believe in Santa Claus. We would spring out of bed with a smile firmly fixed on our faces and in our hearts, eager for the day to start. We would race each other to get in and out of the shower and ready to greet the day, in the hope that we would be the first to arrive at the beautifully wrapped presents waiting for us under life's tree, the ones we had so eagerly been awaiting. There would also likely be a certain air of self-assuredness about us, a confidence in our demeanor and our walk that let the whole world know that we were feeling particularly good about ourselves and the prospects for the day that lay ahead of us. Perhaps if we knew that those around us had received similar messages to start their days, we might even be inclined to let down our guard a bit and share our newfound enthusiasm for life with friend and stranger alike, assured that our kindness would be greeted with the same warm and welcoming smiles with which it was delivered. Most importantly, however, our certainty of the gift to be bestowed on us before the end of the day no doubt would fill us with a joyful restlessness, a profound sense of gleeful anticipation, and more likely than not, a curiosity as to what it would feel like and how we would react when we peeled away just enough of the beautiful wrapping paper on our daily gift to catch that magical first glimpse of the object of our desire.

And yet, part of me wonders just how magical such a life would be. After all, I'm sure each of us can readily identify numerous examples of situations where knowing the outcome ahead of time, no matter how great that outcome turned out to be, almost certainly would have ruined the experience entirely, or at a minimum, significantly dampened the emotions associated with experiencing the event—uncertain but hopeful of a positive outcome. Take, for example, the birth of a first child, the kiss of a first love, the publication of a first book, a first date, riding a bicycle without training wheels, meeting a new best friend, having someone say "I love you" for the first time and truly mean it, a wedding night, receiving praise for a job well done, getting a driver's license or a first car, cashing a first paycheck, even a maiden ride on a new roller coaster. Indeed, one need not look beyond the weekend trip to the movies to appreciate the difference between knowing the ending of the latest suspense thriller before you even walk in the theater and being riveted to the edge of your seat with all of the other moviegoers only to be blindsided by an incredibly creative last-minute plot twist that you never saw coming.

Still other examples, like those involving our favorite teams or athletes in our favorite sports, are often played out on a national or international stage, as was the case in Michael Phelps' historic quest to win 8 gold medals in the Summer Olympics in Beijing, China. I know that, at least from this spectator's point of view, the virtual impossibility of accomplishing that feat and the suspense associated with not knowing the outcome, made each race that much more intriguing and dramatic than the gold medal performance that preceded it.

In fairness, of course, not all such events have the positive outcomes we expect or hope for. To the contrary, many times we are greatly disappointed or worse yet, emotionally or psychologically harmed by the unexpected events that we are confronted with during the day. Sometimes, because of the circumstances in our lives at a given point in time, such "bad outcomes" are almost predictable. It is, I suspect, the potential downside of the uncertainty that is so much a part of all of our lives that, at times, makes us fearful, if not completely unable to get out of bed in the morning, and simultaneously, makes the world I'm imagining (*i.e.*, one in which our day begins with a promise of a favorable outcome) so superficially appealing. And yet, I have come to believe that this is one of life's greatest paradoxes.

The truth is: uncertainty was never intended to be a paralyzing force in our lives. To the contrary, I have come to believe that uncertainty is precisely the gift God intends to give us each morning in the hope that it will motivate us to leap out of bed with a curious, adventuresome, and expectant mind and heart, eager to see what the day holds in store.

Perhaps that something will be a moment in which we catch a glimpse of the magnitude of the gifts with which we have been uniquely blessed, and we will rejoice in that moment. At times, that something most certainly will be disappointment or even heartache. Sometimes, however, even that disappointment will serve as an opportunity or a stepping stone for growth, and on some occasions, reveal a higher good or victory that was there all along, but might not otherwise have been fully appreciated.

Unbeknownst to me at the time, these truths were on display for all the world to see at the 1992 Summer Olympic Games in Barcelona, Spain—a moment best captured by award-winning author Mitch Albom in an August 5, 1992 column entitled "Father, Son Provide Games' Golden Moment" that appeared in the Detroit Free Press—a now-yellowed copy of which has been gathering dust among dozens of similar keepsakes in a file behind my office desk:

BARCELONA, Spain—The son went down as if he had been shot, grabbing his leg, falling to the track. The father, watching from the stands, felt something sink in his stomach. He lowered his head. The memories flashed back: the park near the old house, the boy, 6 years old, racing alongside him, grabbing his body. "Where's the finish line, Dad?" he would say, laughing. "Carry me to the finish line…"

The finish line. The noise of the crowd snapped him back to reality. Cheering? What were they cheering? He looked up to see his son, face twisted in pain, rising to his feet on the red oval track, waving off the medics who carried a stretcher. Derek Redmond, whose Olympic dream was over, whose right hamstring had just snapped, was trying to complete his 400-meter race. He had half that distance to go. Because he couldn't walk, he began to hop. One step. A grimace. Two steps. A yell.

The son was crying.

And the father had to come.

He doesn't really remember all the steps down from Section 131, Row 22, Seat 25 of the Olympic stadium. He doesn't really remember leaping over the railing or landing on the field, or pushing off security guards who were somehow too stunned to stop him. The Olympics? He was not at the Olympics anymore. Jim Redmond was a parent outside a burning house, hearing a cry through the window. And all he knew was, "My son, I had to get to him."

And suddenly, he was alongside him.

"Dad," Derek said, grabbing him, throwing an arm around his shoulder and burying his head to hide the tears. "Dad… get me back to Lane 5. I want to finish."

And leaning on each other, just like the old days, father and son made their way down the track, as the crowd and the whole world watching got this lump in its throat.

You can set the stage for heroism. You can plan your Olympics for maximum exposure, light the skies with fireworks, invite kings and queens and NBA stars. But you can never create the magic of real life.

"If I tried to do that again, I don't think I could," Jim Redmond would admit after this burst of real life was over Monday night, after he had taken his 26-year-old son where his son wanted to go, across the line, where the medical staff once again came running up with a red stretcher.

"No stretcher!" the father barked.

He knew what his son wanted. He had been with him every step of the way, through the good times, when he set the British 400 record, and through the bad times, the four operations on his Achilles' tendon, the countless other injuries that left him unable to run as late as six weeks before these Games.

"Derek's pride was at stake. If he had been taken out on a stretcher he would never have run again. We had agreed, no matter what, that he was going to finish the race. He was going to say that he got through the semifinal of the Olympic 400 meters."

"All he needed was a little support. I am his father. I'm supposed to provide it."

And so he did. And when he was sure his son was OK, when the hamstring had been iced and the tears had dried, Jim Redmond slowly made his way back to his seat, stopping to apologize to every official along the way, because, as he would put it, "I didn't want the British to get a bad name for disrupting the Olympics."

You couldn't make up a story like this. Back in North Hamptonshire, in the small village they call home, Jim Redmond's wife, daughter and son-in-law were watching on TV. The daughter, nine months pregnant, saw her brother crying in pain, then saw her father, filling up the screen, the crowd rising to applaud him—Dad? On the track? Apparently, this was all too much. She felt this sudden pain. Next thing you know, the doctor was at the door, ready to deliver a baby.

As it turned out, that was a false alarm. But the idea was so wonderfully real. Right here, in an Olympics weighted down with commercialism, drug rumors, its own largess, here we have a plain old family in a plain old town that seems so tied into one another; when one feels pain, the other twinges. And goes to help. Even if it means leaping onto the Olympic track.

Jim Redmond is almost 50 years old. Two decades ago, he started the business he still owns. A machine shop called "J. Redmond & Sons."

"I had hoped Derek would take over, but he has other ideas. That's OK. He's a good kid. He keeps my name clean. You can't ask for more than that."

Or more than this, maybe the best story of the 1992 Games. Like most Olympians, Derek Redmond came here dreaming of gold, the fantasy, the end of the rainbow. Instead, he got his own backyard. There they were again, arm in arm, headed for the finish line: J. Redmond & Son, together as usual.

Come to think of it, what could be more golden?[2]

Dear Ashley,

If my personal experience over the years is any indication, 9 out of 10 people who learn Derek Redmond's story, either by reading about it or seeing a video replay of the event, have the same reaction—none can find anything positive to say about it. Instead, they view it as a tragedy of sorts, a graphic and painful example of just how cruel and unfair life can be. They shudder to think of how Derek (and his dad) must have felt, knowing that, in an instant, his entire life's work had been ruined, some might even suggest rendered a complete waste of time, by something as fickle and unpredictable as a pulled muscle. To the extent that's truly all they see, however, I believe they badly miss the point of the story.

Don't get me wrong. I know from reading interviews that Derek and his father have given over the years that both shared similar emotions in the grip of that very disappointing moment. It would be impossible not to. But I also suspect that, in the quiet hours and days that followed, a very different reality emerged, particularly for Derek. Like most people who are fortunate enough to find and pursue their passion, Derek Redmond didn't need an Olympic gold medal or even a silver or a bronze medal to validate him or his abilities, nor did he need them to justify his life-long commitment to running—though any one of those medals certainly would have been a welcomed guest in a trophy cabinet that already included dozens of national and world class medals and awards.

2   Reprinted with permission from Mitch Albom and The Detroit Free Press.

The only thing Derek Redmond needed to be "complete" was to finish what, unbeknownst to him at the time, was to be the final race in the journey he had begun as a young boy so many years earlier, which, of course, is precisely what he did in fairly dramatic fashion. Why?—because Derek Redmond was passionate about running. It was what motivated him, what enabled him to dream, what made each day a new challenge, what brought him joy, what inspired him. He knew, perhaps better than most who shared his gift, that from time to time, he would suffer injuries— some of which would make it impossible for him to compete—and yet he kept running, all the way to the Olympic Games, literally within a few hundred yards of being able to say that he was one of the top eight sprinters in the world.

Perhaps if he had known when he started running what the final chapter of his sprinting career would look like, Derek Redmond never would have gotten into the starting blocks at all. Fortunately for those of us who stand to learn and benefit from his (and his dad's) commitment, he didn't know the end of the story before it began. And the same is true for us. My hope is that you will find your passion, and when you do, that you will eagerly embrace it and the opportunity that each new day affords to continue to pursue it down wherever its sometimes straight, sometimes winding, often wildly unpredictable, but always intriguing and challenging trail may lead. Know as you do, that should you ever stumble, as you most likely will from time to time along the way, you can always lean on me to continue your quest to finish the race.

With All My Love,
Dad

CHAPTER 19

The Gorilla®

(Embracing the sometimes jagged, often
ill-fitting pieces of the puzzles of our lives)

I'm not entirely sure what it is about the human psyche that causes us to think in such a manner, but my sense is that most people view their life journeys in very linear and compartmentalized terms. Not unlike "The Game of Life®," we proceed, in lock-step fashion, along the path that we believe we are expected or perhaps even pre-destined to follow. We begin our journey in childhood, where others, hopefully much wiser than us and with our best interests in mind, make most of the significant decisions for us. Before long, we transition into adolescence and young adulthood, where, with appropriate guidance, we likely start to make some of our own choices and learn to accept the consequences associated with them—good and bad. From there, it seems like a relatively small step to the next logical square on the board—the actual starting point of the 1860-vintage board game—when we choose to "go to college" or, alternatively, to "begin a career."

Soon after, we find ourselves confronted with the usual next steps—each of which, not unlike their board game counterparts, carry with them certain labels, privileges, obligations and expectations. We marry (becoming husbands and wives); get a job (becoming teachers, ministers, doctors, lawyers, therapists, etc.), have children and do our level-best to raise them (becoming moms and dads); pursue various avocations and hobbies (becoming coaches, classroom helpers, artists, writers, musicians, etc.); retire; grow old; and, well, you know, the "Game Over" part. At times, we occupy spaces and inherit labels that we neither expect, want or feel we deserve (*e.g.*, we become caretaker, patient, addict, eating disorder sufferer, accident or crime victim, widow, divorcee, cancer survivor, etc.). And yet, invariably, we keep moving, often without giving much conscious thought to where we've been or where we may be going. Instead, we focus exclusively on the "space" in which we find ourselves and the immediate decisions and consequences that occupying it entails. In essence, we "are" where we land.

The problems associated with this board-game-like approach to life are many. Principal among them, however, is the inescapable reality that allowing where we are or what label may be attached to us at any particular point in time to define who we are can leave us feeling stuck—disconnected from what has come before. It also renders us incapable of fully embracing and experiencing all that the present has to offer and makes it difficult to visualize a future filled with the possibility, if not the promise, that one day we will realize the true desires of our heart. Finally, but no less significantly, it obscures our ability to see how all of the sometimes jagged, often seemingly ill-fitting pieces of our lives operate together to form the mosaic that makes each of us unique.

I was first introduced to these potentially life-changing concepts by, of all things, a gorilla! True, it was not just any gorilla. It was The Gorilla®—the ground-breaking mascot of the NBA's Phoenix Suns, who, for more than eight seasons (from 1980 to 1988), roamed the hardwoods of Veterans Memorial Coliseum, entertaining, poking fun at, amusing and engaging audiences, players and coaches alike with a unique repertoire of sideline and on-court humor, antics, and dance routines that set the standard for what ultimately would become the role occupied by mascots in basketball and many other modern-day sports. By the time we met, Henry Rojas, the man behind the mask, had long since retired his gorilla costume and was serving as the Spiritual Director at a prominent residential treatment facility for those suffering from eating disorders. It was Family Week. We and our daughter, together with dozens of other similarly-situated families, were gathered in a small chapel in a remote part of the country. Suffice it to say, we were a far cry from the audiences Henry had grown accustomed to entertaining, but it was immediately clear to me that he was precisely where he wanted (and we needed) him to be.

Henry began his remarks by recounting stories from a childhood that some might characterize as rather unremarkable, if not undirected. At school, Henry was often disruptive, the quintessential "class clown." In fact, on more than one occasion, Henry's exasperated (though likely equally amused!) teachers struck deals with Henry, allowing him to "have the floor" for uninterrupted "cut-up time" during the first five minutes of the class day, in exchange for a promise that he would behave for the rest. Henry's mischievous but often entertaining personality was also evident at home, where his sisters regularly included Henry in their "dress up" re-creations of daily soap operas, while others, including his parents, often relied on Henry and his enthusiasm for singing and dancing as a source of amusement on demand at large family gatherings. Henry recalled not really having a sense of what he wanted to do with his life as he was growing up—save for a desire of the heart to one day play in the National Basketball Association (NBA)—a desire which, despite Henry's life-long love of the game and his relative proficiency in playing, didn't seem very likely given what ultimately would become Henry's 5' 9 3/4" frame (<u>Note</u>: Henry insisted that I be very precise about this!).

Then one day, Henry received a call from his sister who at the time was working for Eastern Onion, a singing telegram service in the Phoenix area. She asked Henry if he would be interested in helping her out of a bind caused by an employee's last-minute inability to deliver a singing telegram to a fan at that evening's Phoenix Suns' game. Seizing upon what seemed like an excellent opportunity to see the Suns play "for a song," Henry readily agreed to help, only to be told moments later that there was a small catch: Henry would have to deliver the telegram in a gorilla suit! Despite his best efforts to beg out, Henry ultimately relented and followed his sister's instructions as to where to meet security personnel to gain access to the auditorium, and ultimately where to find the fan who was to have been the intended recipient of the telegram. When the fan didn't show up, Henry, still dressed in the gorilla costume, settled into a seat a few rows up from the court, intending to watch the game until the next time-out, before hurriedly finding the closest exit and making his escape.

When the time-out whistle blew, Henry took a few steps toward the court and began to make his way around the perimeter to a nearby exit. As he neared the basket at one end of the court, the high-energy music that the Suns used to entertain fans during time-outs started to blare from the loudspeakers. Henry froze. Though to this day he is still unsure what possessed him to do so, Henry slowly moved onto the court, and as he had done so many times for friends and relatives as a young child, he began to dance! The crowd went berserk! When the music stopped, Henry headed for the exit, certain that he would be apprehended by the two security officers that now stood in front of the previously unobstructed doors. To his surprise, however, they were there to convey an unexpected and soon-to-be life-altering message from the Suns' executive box: "See if the gorilla will agree to stay for the rest of the game and perform during the remaining time-outs!"

The rest, as they say, is history. The following morning, Henry's (The Gorilla®'s) face was splashed across the front page of the local sports pages, and within days, the Suns had signed Henry to a lucrative contract to serve as the team's (and the NBA's) first and still most recognizable mascot. Despite his size and likely when he least expected it, Henry Rojas had made it to the NBA—albeit not in the way he may have envisioned "playing" there when he was that shy, sensitive young man, desperately searching for his identity. In fact, he not only made it to the NBA, he went on to star in two NBA All-Star games, and ultimately was inducted into the Hall of Fame—the Mascot Hall of Fame, of course! In the process, Henry had realized one of the childhood desires of his heart. More importantly perhaps, along the way he discovered several principles that are critically important ingredients in fertilizing the seed of hope:

Our lives are not comprised of a series of isolated events (like the neatly-bordered squares on a board game), nor are we (or should we allow ourselves to be) defined by any one of those events or by the labels and meanings that we or others may attach to those seemingly discrete occurrences. Instead, while we may not understand or fully appreciate their relevance to the bigger picture at the time, the things that we do, the choices that we make (or fail to make), the manner in which our unique personalities manifest themselves, the personal challenges we are asked to endure at various stages in our lives are part of a collection of stories, which, laid one on top of the other, ultimately contribute something to the whole of who we are, to where we've been and to where we're going.

Consciously or subconsciously, many of the significant others in Henry's life (*e.g.*, teachers, coaches, friends, relatives, etc.) likely were quick to label him, based on his behaviors, various aspects of his personality and his physical appearance, in limiting and at times, unflattering if not hurtful ways—he was "the funny guy," the "class clown," the "cut-up," the "unfocused one," the "short guy," etc.—and he, in turn, undoubtedly adopted some or all of those descriptions of self, together with the expectations and limitations that went with them along the way. Unbeknownst to Henry at the time, however, God too was watching his personality unfold and He was drawing on those same events and fashioning them, using them in a way and for a good that no one, even Henry, likely could or would have ever imagined!

In fact, sitting in that small chapel that incredibly hot summer afternoon, it was evident to me that even though Henry has long since taken off the mask that once gave him the freedom he felt he needed to more fully express himself, God is still doing that in Henry's life, not only for his benefit, but for the benefit of all who are privileged to hear him speak. More importantly, Henry's unique life experiences carry with them the promise that, if allowed to do so, God will gladly do the same in each of our lives in the hope that one day all of us will come to realize one of the guiding principles by which He intended "the real game of life" to be played: with a conviction that we are worthy, that we are capable, that we are perfect in spirit, that we are completely free and that we (and all of the idiosyncrasies that go along with who we are) are loved beyond all measure.

Dear Ashley,

In the silence that I try to make my pre-bedtime routine, this simple thought came to my heart last night: each of us has been blessed with the wisdom, the courage and the inner strength necessary to write a unique and compelling life story—one that is filled with adventure, curiosity, self-discovery, giving, friendship, fun and love. I encourage you to open your heart to that reality and to fully embrace the journey that almost certainly will accompany the writing of the story of your own life, with all of its ups and downs, its twists and turns, its joys and heartaches, its mysteries and uncertainties. As part of that journey, I also urge you to dedicate (and constantly re-dedicate) yourself to maintaining the spiritual, physical and emotional health of the writer of that story—YOU! Learn and draw strength from your yesterdays and then turn the page. While they are an integral part of your story, they are only a part and by no means the rest of it. Focus, instead, clearly (and with a grateful heart) on the unique gift that today represents. It is (if you will allow it to be) a new beginning, another step on life's journey. Take a deep breath, search your soul and identify the desires of your heart and then, when you're ready, pick up your pen and write—with faith, with hope and with love.

With All My Love,
Dad

CHAPTER 20

Chuck

(Giving is living)

I n his 1964 classic, *The Giving Tree*, award-winning author and poet Shel Silverstein uses a story about an unlikely relationship between a boy and a tree to capture two principles that I have come to believe are fundamental and essential ingredients in the recipe for a full and rewarding life, namely: (1) a willingness to give of ourselves to others selflessly and completely, without any expectation that our giving will be acknowledged, let alone reciprocated; and (2) a corresponding vulnerability and openness that allows us to be aware of and ultimately to fully experience the selfless giving of others.

The story begins innocently enough—a young boy playfully enjoying all that the outdoors has to offer, and in the process, finding a friend in the form of a favorite tree. The tree enthusiastically embraces and returns the boy's affection by generously giving of herself in the form of leaves for a crown fit for the "King of the Forest," apples to provide sustenance, branches for climbing and swinging, and ultimately when the day is done, shade for some much-needed rest. Initially, her generosity and her gifts are reciprocated—both in the attention that the boy pays to the tree ("every day the boy would come") and in his warm embraces ("the boy loved the tree—very much. And, the tree was happy!").

As the boy grows older, however, he becomes increasingly less interested in the simple pleasures he once enjoyed and shared with the tree. His curious and playful spirit is trampled upon by the demands and busyness of everyday life, and over time, is replaced with a self-centered and demanding heart that is indifferent to the tree's existence—save for the extent to which he might be able to use the tree to acquire the material things and relationships he grows to covet: money, a house, a spouse—even children. In spite of her not-so-young-anymore-friend's cold indifference, the tree continues to give, first urging the "boy" to sell the entirety of her harvest of apples, and eventually insisting that he strip her of her very branches and use them to build a home. Each time, all that the tree desires in return is that the boy use her gifts to secure the happiness she so longs for him to have. But each time, after an extended absence, the boy returns a little older, a little sadder and a little more tired. At one point, the boy, now a grumpy old man, seeks a means of escaping it all—as if he could run from what he has become—and though it most certainly breaks her heart to do so, the tree willingly gives what little she has left, her trunk, so that he can build a boat and sail away—and, hopefully, finally, maybe be happy!

Although he was gone for quite some time, eventually, virtually on death's doorstep, the boy returns for what will likely be his final visit. In spite of all she had done for the boy, often at considerable sacrifice to herself, the tree's only regret, indeed, her lament, was that she had nothing left to offer, nothing left to give. There were no more leaves for crowning, no more branches for swinging, no more apples for eating, and no more trunks for climbing. All she had left was a stump, which, of course, was precisely what her then bone-weary friend needed most—a place to sit and rest, to remember and reflect on a simpler time—a happy, more carefree time. Most of all, it was a place to reconnect with an old friend who never stopped giving, and, in the process, give her what she had always longed for most—time spent in the company of a friend, who, likely for the first time since his days as "King of the Forest," was finally happy and at peace.

Suffice it to say, the advertising and marketing executives who fill the boardrooms on Madison Avenue have no interest in having their customers, especially those who are young and impressionable, find Silverstein's little green gem, let alone embrace the mindset of his fictional tree. They would just as soon it remain buried and mostly forgotten on the bookshelves of neighborhood bookstores and middle and high school libraries. They know that their livelihood, if not their very existence, depends on our becoming and remaining fixated on the me and not just any "me"—a me they've carefully created and aggressively promote, often through disturbingly misleading billboard, television and print advertising, a me that is ever-changing, elusive and intentionally unattainable. It is a highly superficial, frequently airbrush-enhanced "me" that we (and, more importantly, our young adults) are told holds the key to our happiness—a happiness they insist is within our reach, so long as we are willing to purchase the treasure trove of health and beauty aids necessary to achieve it (*e.g.*, designer label clothing and shoes, glamorous hair styles and the hair care products necessary to maintain them, make-up and skin care regimens, dietary foods and supplements, etc.).

Many believe that, at least initially, the quest to be like the Madison Avenue model is one of the principal triggers to a life of disordered eating, particularly among middle, high school and college-age women—and those researchers and commentators may well be right. What I find interesting, however, is that, paradoxically, the eating disorder voice depends on a curiously similar, albeit far more dangerous paradigm for its existence. Like Madison Avenue, the eating disorder voice insists on its target audience remaining fiercely loyal to, if not obsessed with, an equally distorted, mostly unattainable image of self—an image, which at least in those suffering from anorexia, is almost wholly defined by the sufferer's gross misperception of her daily, if not hourly, reflections in a mirror. It is a world view that is disturbingly myopic in that it focuses solely on the me to the exclusion of almost everything and everyone else. Indeed, the ability of the eating disorder voice to take root and thrive depends on the sufferer disconnecting and becoming isolated from that which, I believe, all human hearts long for most: companionship, community and the ability to share our gifts and our lives with others and to embrace the gifts that others share with us.

Silverstein's fictional tree is there to remind all of us in a simplistic, "user-friendly" way that at the end of the day, our true beauty, our self-worth and the fullness of our life is determined not by how we look, what we possess or how we compare, physically or otherwise, to those around us, but rather by the extent to which we empty ourselves in serving others. The fact is: the "giving tree" could have been the most magnificent apple tree in the entire orchard. Its trunk could have been sturdy and straight—perfect for climbing. Its branches could have been especially well-proportioned and strong—perfect for swinging. Its leaves could have been lush, exquisitely defined and brightly colored— perfect for weaving into a crown. Its fruit could have been plentiful and delicious—ideal for a mid-afternoon snack. Its canopy could have cast a broad net of shade—a welcome respite from the hot summer sun. And yet, without the boy, without the ability to share, lovingly, selflessly, unhesitatingly all that it had to give with him and without the boy's corresponding willingness to accept and embrace those gifts, even if it wasn't always with an appropriately grateful heart, it would have been just another tree blowing in the wind, subjected to the vagaries of the elements of nature—destined, like all of the other trees in the forest, to live out its life, wither away and die. As it was, however, its life was full, its joy abundant, and its message clear: each of us is an integral part of a potentially wonderful whole, a whole that depends on our willingness to share and our acceptance of the sharing of others. We would do well to "be the tree."

Dear Ashley,

I want to share a letter I wrote to my friend, Chuck, on what turned out to be the eve of his death. While he died much too young and there is a tremendous amount of sadness around that inexplicable reality, in my mind (and I think in his), Chuck lived a full life. It was full, in large measure, because I suspect at a very early age, perhaps through his faith, his upbringing, and his having been witness to living examples like the person he would ultimately become, Chuck came to understand that a full life depends on emptying oneself to others in a selfless way. I only wish I had openly shared my appreciation with him and for him sooner than I did:

January 13, 2005

Dear Chuck,

This note is long overdue and I apologize for that. I'm not sure why it is that we men have such difficulty sharing our feelings for another. I'm sure it has something to do with the messages we receive as young boys, messages that are only reinforced as we get older and enter the work world. The idea that we're different from girls— that we're supposed to be tough, to always be in control of our emotions, that we aren't supposed to cry, that crying is a sign of weakness, that tears somehow make us less of a man. I never really bought into all of those beliefs, which probably is why, much to Cyndy's chagrin at times, I spent most of my young-adult and adult life hanging out with friends who were women, and in the process, have spilled more tears along the way than I care to think about. Still, I'm certain that those messages had an impact on me, because to this day, I struggle to be open and vulnerable with other men. I need to do better about that. Perhaps this note will be a starting point.

There are a lot of things that I want you to know, things that I know I should have told you along the way, but for one reason or another, never felt that the time was right to share them, or if the time was right, never was able to summon the courage to break through the male barriers that inevitably go up whenever two guys find themselves alone together. Seems like it's always a lot easier to talk about work, sports, politics, finances, the kids, etc., than it is to share our fears, our concerns, our feelings towards others or towards each other, our aspirations, our faith, our hopes, our disappointments. I suppose part of it is that we know how much each other is already dealing with, between being the head of a family, the principal breadwinner, a father, a husband, a handyman, and we are reluctant to add our own problems to each other's plate. I'm as guilty of that as the next guy, just as I am of believing, like most men do, that when problems arise, we should just tough 'em out. Of course, you and I know it doesn't work that way.

First things first, I want you to know how much I have cherished you and our friendship over the years. From the early days, when you were thoughtful enough to install a gate in your backyard so that our children and our families would have one less obstacle to overcome in spending time together, I knew that you were a special person—and I was right. You were and are, in the words of a therapist friend of mine from Dallas, a "New Father," a man who was and is far more concerned with finding out how you could find more time to spend with your family than you were with finding excuses to spend more time at the office; a man who has always been other-centered; a man of faith and of service; a man who would readily drop whatever he was doing to help a friend, a neighbor, or a business associate in need or simply to listen; and, above all else, a man of principle, of integrity, of character, of commitment. I have always admired you for all of those gifts and am eternally grateful for all that they have contributed to my life, and by your example, the lives of our children.

I also want you to know that I have always admired your commitment and your love for Robert and Katie. Dads don't always get a lot of credit for those things and certainly when our children are young, they can't possibly appreciate how much energy and sacrifice that kind of a commitment requires, but as a dad myself, I do and someday they will too. You've always been there for your family—at every school or church function in which they participated, at every softball and baseball game (more often than not in the dugout!), pool-side at every swim meet, greenside at golf tournaments and high school matches, even in things as simple as family meals, outings, and vacations. In being there, you have given your children a gift more magnificent than even they realize— the gift of you, the gift of your presence, and all that those gifts signify. However, I also have seen firsthand and have been deeply touched by the emotional energy and love you have invested in their lives behind the scenes—a type of being there that they will never see, but one that I saw and admire greatly. You are and have been an exceptional role model for your children and for other dads, including me, whose paths you have crossed along the way.

I also admire and more often than you will ever know have been very moved by your relationship with Libby. I know from our conversations over the years how committed you are to her and how much you love her. I also know from watching the two of you interact over the years how much she loves you. I can tell you that your commitment to each other, even in the face of what certainly must have been some difficult times over the years, has always been a positive influence on my relationship with Cyndy. In an era where the institution of marriage seems to have lost its luster, it's refreshing and encouraging to know that there are those like you and Libby who still understand and respect the sacrifice and hard work that the marital commitment requires. Your and Libby's level of devotion to each other has set a wonderful example for Robert and Katie, as well as for Greg and Ashley. I am grateful for that. I also am grateful for the times that you trusted me enough as a friend to share your thoughts and feelings about Libby and your marriage, as well as the times when you cared enough to listen and offer your heartfelt concern and advice about my relationship with Cyndy.

Chuck, I know that you and Libby have been confronted with the greatest challenge of your lives. As I have told Libby many times, I wish that there was something I could do to ease your burden. Unfortunately, all I have to offer are my thoughts, my prayers and my friendship, which have been there from the beginning and which I will continue to offer. In the meantime, I want you to know that you are truly a remarkable person and that I consider myself blessed many times over to have the privilege of calling you my friend.

With love and concern,
Don

I am forever grateful to Chuck for reminding me by his example that truly living means selflessly giving every chance we get.

With All My Love,
Dad

CHAPTER 21

The TPD³

(Taking a closer look at the "Total Package Dad")

While I had hoped to avoid the subject for reasons that will become apparent in a moment, my sense is that no book that attempts to tackle the subject of eating disorders would be complete without some discussion of body image. So, here are my 2.5 cents on the subject:

I have a really BIG HEAD. I'm not talking about big in an egocentric, swollen kind of way. I'm talking about geometrically disproportionate-to-the-rest-of-my-body big. I'm talking about make-a-child-party-hat-look-like-the-size-of-a-snow-cone-cup-on-a-basketball big. I'm talking about don't-bother-trying-to-buy-me-a-hat-because-it-will-never-fit big. For as long as I can remember, this very prominent and unalterable physical feature has resulted in my being the butt of all kinds of jokes and name-calling by classmates,

---

3   "TPD" is a term of affection (I think!) that my children often used to refer to me—ironically, given what you're about to read, because of the many different hats I wore when they were growing up.

friends, colleagues, members of my own family and others. If there's a derogatory or even remotely humorous comment to be made or a name to call people with unusually large heads, chances are I've heard it or been called it at one time or another. You name it, I've been called it: "Bucket-head," "Neo-noggin" (as in Neolithic), "Mr. Potato Head," "Charlie Brown" and the ever popular "Pumpkin-head." In the beginning, I was terribly self-conscious and embarrassed by the sheer size of my head—not to mention hurt by the many comments and jokes about it.

Over time, I've learned to roll with it, to try not to take the remarks too personally. Occasionally, I'll even join in the "fun" by exaggerating the difficulty I have putting on a fully-expanded golf cap (I've learned to wear visors instead) or making a point of stopping by the hat counter and trying on one style after another just to prove the obvious—I have a HUGE HEAD! Truth is, however, the size of my head is one of the reasons I have never spent very much time staring at myself in the mirror, but it is by no means the only reason.

You see, as if my gargantuan head were not bad enough, I'm also one of the only people on the planet to have been born with an upside-down smile. I wish I were kidding, but I'm not. No matter how hard I laugh or how hard I try, I simply cannot make the ends of my mouth form a normal smile. Believe me, I've tried everything imaginable. In fact, when my friends first started making fun of my smile, I would stand in front of the mirror at night, sometimes for hours at a time, and physically prop up the ends of my mouth—in the hope that I could train them to go where normal lips go when they smile. No such luck. For a period of time, I actually convinced myself that I would even be content if my lips simply remained neutral when I was trying to smile (*i.e.*, if they stayed straight across, rather than wilted, in response to an uproariously funny joke). Try as I might, that wasn't happening either. To make matters even more awkward, invariably those who saw my unusual smile for the first time would ask why I smiled upside down, assuming, I suppose, that I had a choice in the matter. I always wondered how I should answer that question. The obvious answer, of course, as in the case of my GINORMOUS HEAD, is that "I was born this way." But, on more than one occasion, I thought it might be far more interesting to suggest that I once had a normal smile, but that over time, the profound sense of sadness that set in every time someone commented on my admittedly unusual appearance had eroded the ends of my lips to the point that they no longer had any interest in returning to their original and intended upright position. Somehow I never found the courage to play that card, choosing instead to simply absorb the quirky stares and often unintentionally harmful comments. My smile is yet another reason I don't spend much time in front of the mirror.

And then there's the small issue relating to my ears. Admittedly, this problem is not quite as obvious as the head size and the upside-down smile, but it is made far more apparent than it otherwise would be by virtue of the fact that I have been wearing glasses since I was 12 years old. What's the problem, you ask? The problem is that one of my ears is slightly lower than the other. Not that big a deal, right? Wrong. From the standpoint of appearance and overall attractiveness, it is a big deal, particularly for someone who needs to wear glasses, because, as I came to realize, in order for glasses to appear level to the rest of the world, your ears have to be level. When they aren't, no matter how skillful the optician and his staff are at adjusting your frames, there is simply no way to get them to sit level and function optimally. Consequently, my glasses, like my smile, have always been a bit on the crooked side, not a good combination when you consider the fact that they are attached to a head whose sheer enormity commands immediate scrutiny by everyone I meet.

Again, there is nothing I can do to improve this by-product of birth, much in the same way that there is no way to change the fact that one of my legs is shorter than the other, that one of my eyebrows is higher than the other or that my shoulders are more than a little on the relaxed side, as opposed to being squared as I've repeatedly been told "they should be." Still, at the end of the day, all of these "deficiencies" are simply physical parts of who I am that I'm forced to live with, recognizing, of course, that there are real-life consequences attached to them—not the least of which is that, next year, they likely will account for my being left off of People Magazine's "100 Most Beautiful People" list for what will be the 54th consecutive time!

Don't get me wrong. I'm not suggesting for a minute that my anatomical eccentricities compare in magnitude or complexity with the body image issues that are such an integral part of eating disorders and, to a lesser extent, the daily lives of many women—young and old. I'm also not naïve enough to believe that, as a man, I will ever fully understand the unique challenges associated with those issues. Having listened to my daughter and dozens of other similarly afflicted, as well as unafflicted, women share on the subject over the last several years, I know better. Moreover, in poking fun at myself, as I have done to a large extent in this chapter, I don't mean to trivialize body image issues or the obvious power they have to influence the lives and behaviors of those afflicted with such disorders. I am, however, convinced that the path to true happiness and, in the case of those in the grip of eating disorders, the first step on the road to recovery depends on our willingness and ability to care less about the reflection we see in the bathroom mirror each morning and more about the reflections we create in the sometimes radiant, often tear-filled eyes of those whose lives we touch with gifts that will never be captured by a mirror—gifts of friendship, kindness, trust, compassion, empathy, encouragement, understanding—even the simple gift of our mere presence and our willingness to listen.

How can I be so certain? I'm certain because I've had the opportunity and privilege to see those reflections dozens of times in my own life—and, not surprisingly, none of them had anything to do with the size of my head, the shape of my smile, the levelness of my ears, the length of my legs, the proportionality of my eyebrows or my weight, which, at times, fluctuates like the New York Stock Exchange. Most recently, I saw them in the dying eyes of a childhood best friend, who, despite our having fallen out of touch for nearly thirty years, was moved to tears and comforted in his final days simply by my taking the time to visit him in the hospital, to hold his hand, to thank him for his friendship so many years ago, when, unbeknownst to him, I too desperately needed companionship, and to offer to help him hoist a small juice box to his lips so that he could quench his thirst.

I've also seen the reflection in the frightened gaze of a 10-year-old little leaguer whom I coached many years ago, when, after noticing that tears had started to well up in his eyes, I cared enough to call time-out—first to simply ask if something was wrong and then upon learning that moments before the game, his mom and dad had told him they were getting a divorce, to offer quiet assurances from a coach he knew he could trust that somehow, someday "everything would be all right."

I also know it because I felt it in the warmth of a spontaneous hug I received from the "Young Mother of Two" in Chapter 17, a complete stranger to me at the time, only moments after I uttered a few simple words of affirmation delivered from the heart upon hearing her incredible story—words that told her through the tears that were streaming down my face that although I had just met her, I already greatly admired her courage and her strength, and contrary to her lifelong but no less heart-breaking self-belief, was convinced that she was quite worthy of living. Should I go on?

Should I mention that I was the coach who whispered a few words of hope and encouragement to Travis (Chapter 8), and by that simple act, helped to create an opportunity for him to learn that sometimes overcoming the fear of failure only requires taking the smallest of first steps (*e.g.*, a bunt)? Should I confess that, while I missed it at the time, I'm just as certain the reflection was there to be seen in Travis's eyes as he stood heroically on first base watching the winning run cross home plate.

Or would it better make the point if I told you I had seen the reflection in the no-longer-downcast eyes of a beautiful aspiring young writer, who, having just laid her soul bare to a group of complete strangers by reciting a gut-wrenching poem she'd written about her own eating disorder struggle, heard, perhaps for the first time, that she had a very special gift with words and the power to use them to touch and change other people's lives.

In fact, the more I think about it, the clearer it becomes that although I likely wasn't paying much attention to it at the time, I have seen the reflection over and over again—or at least it was there to be seen—as it undoubtedly was for the real and fictional characters whose stories are recounted in this book. It's not hard to imagine it in the case of Jim and Derek Redmond, The Girl on the Park Bench and her patient tutor, Bagger Vance and Junnah, Coach Taylor and Brock, Courtney and her San Francisco Ballet colleague, Coach John Harding and Timothy Noble, Dr. Mac and his patients, the Miners and their rescuers, the Tree and the little boy, the Little Blue Engine and the children on the other side of the mountain—to name a few. Indeed, if you look closely enough (I have; it's there), you might even see it in the photograph on the cover of this book.

What is most important to me, however, is that YOU see it—or at least entertain and then act on the idea of searching for it in your life. Because, I promise you this: if you will embrace the inescapable reality that I know to be true about you, even though you and I have never met (*i.e.*, that you are not the person you perceive or misperceive yourself to be in the bathroom mirror any more than I am), you will see it—time and time again—and it may just change your life.

EPILOGUE

Throughout the ages, Biblical scholars, theologians and philosophers have reflected and commented on what they perceive to be the innate longing of the human heart to believe in and ultimately connect with a higher power—a God that is all-loving, benevolent, merciful and at least open to meeting the heart's innermost needs and desires. At one time or another, whether we ultimately choose to embrace it or not, I suspect most of us have experienced that longing. I know I have.

But I also have come to appreciate, both through my own experiences and in listening attentively to the brutally honest and often heart-wrenching testimony of others, that there is an equally powerful inclination of the human heart, particularly a heart that has been (or still is being) ravaged by loneliness, abuse, neglect, rejection, disrespect, trauma, humiliation, a fundamental breach of trust, a sense of hopelessness, illness, guilt, grief, despair, feelings of inadequacy and worthlessness, betrayal and shame, namely to conclude that there either is no God, or worse yet, that He does exist but has chosen to abandon us in our hour of need because, our hearts imagine, we are no more worthy of His love and compassion than we are of anyone else's.

Such inclinations are not reserved for those whose faith and belief system were weak before the onset of the storms that shake them to their core. What is equally indisputable is the enormity of the void created by that perception in a heart more desperate than ever for a reason to survive. It is an unimaginably lonely and hopeless place to be—I know, because I've been there more times than I care to think about over the last several years, as has my daughter and countless others whose paths she crossed in the course of her treatment.

Largely as a result of the fictional and non-fictional people and events that fill the pages of this book, however, I ultimately found it impossible to continue to cling to either of those wholly unfulfilling possibilities (*i.e.*, that God either does not exist, or if He does, that He is far from loving or compassionate). I simply cannot believe, even in the midst of what at times has been almost unbearable heartache and suffering, that all I have seen and heard is simply random, or even more disturbingly, that it is some intentional form of Divine punishment. To the contrary, my experiences have led me to conclude that none of this makes any sense at all in the absence of a loving God. This is not to say that I am any closer to putting the pieces of this incredibly complex and often seemingly irrational puzzle together, let alone solving it. I'm not. I'm also not prepared to suggest that there still aren't times when I doubt myself, my faith in God and my belief in the fundamental goodness, courageousness, hopefulness and selflessness that resides in all of us. There are. More importantly, if I'm to be honest with myself and with you, I can't pretend that the wounds exposed in this book have fully healed or that I or my daughter have successfully overcome all of the challenges borne of the last several years—they and we haven't. I'm not naïve enough to believe that considerable obstacles don't lie ahead—they almost certainly do.

Instead, it simply means that somewhere along the way, I made a conscious choice similar to one made and shared with me by a close friend in one of my darkest hours. He presented it this way: "Don, there either is a God or there isn't. I choose to believe that there is." In doing so, I embarked on what I suspect will now be a lifelong scavenger hunt of sorts—one devoted not to dwelling on events that misconstrued could easily disprove His existence. Instead, I embarked on one filled with a heart open to the possibility that He does exist and with a heightened sensitivity to uncovering the many subtle ways in which I believe He is eagerly trying to make His existence and presence known to all of us, hopeful that along the way, I will catch tiny glimpses into the fullness of life He intended each of us to experience. I invite you to join me on this exciting and highly unpredictable journey.

THE END

(Well—not quite)

Dear Ashley,

...here is the deepest secret nobody knows
here is the root of the root and the bud of the bud
and the sky of the sky of a tree called life;
which grows higher than the soul can hope or mind can hide
and this is the wonder that's keeping the stars apart—
i carry your heart (i carry it in my heart)[4]

---

4   excerpt from "i carry your heart" by ee cummings.

APPENDIX

For those who are so inclined, the following source materials are offered as additional points of reflection on the themes addressed in each of the Chapters:

THE HURT
Chapter 1: On Loneliness and Intimacy
("Dealing with it just like all the other kids"—or not)
Suggested Reading: *The Little Prince* by Antoine De Saint-Exupéry
Suggested Viewing: *The Greatest Game Ever Played* (2005)
Suggested Listening: "The Baseball Song" by Bob Bennett http://www.youtube.com/watch?v=A90XZ5GWYKQ

Chapter 2: Daddy's Little Girl
(Walking unsuspectingly in our father's footsteps)
Suggested Viewing: *On Golden Pond* (1981) and
Father and Daughter by Nikos Déjà Vu http://www.youtube.com/watch?v=MgdsfRDxIeQ
Suggested Reading: *Our Fathers, Ourselves* by Dr. Peggy Drexler

Suggested Listening: "My Little Girl" by Tim McGraw http://www.youtube.com/watch?v=9I5UV4VWCSk

Chapter 3: Brittany
(Living in an "if you ain't first, you're last" world)
Suggested Viewing: *Searching for Bobby Fischer* (1993)
Suggested Reading: *The Overachievers* by Alexandra Robbins
Suggested Listening: "The First Cut is the Deepest" by Sheryl Crow http://www.youtube.com/watch?v=-VfmxlTa9gg&feature=related

Chapter 4: The Girl at Detroit Metropolitan Airport
(Turning a deaf ear to the sometimes silent, sometimes not-so-silent tears of those we love)
Suggested Reading: *Listening to the Littlest* by Ruth Reardon
Suggested Listening: "When She Cries" by Britt Nicole http://www.youtube.com/watch?v=7llFVOad-DM&feature=related and "Hold My Heart" by Sara Bareilles http://www.youtube.com/watch?v=L7f12Hjz7mA

Chapter 5: The Gift of Imperfection
(Maybe being perfect isn't all it's cracked up to be)
Suggested Reading: *The Missing Piece* by Shel Silverstein
Suggested Listening: "Imperfect is the New Perfect" by Caitlin Crosby http://www.youtube.com/watch?v=Fli8UpFcpQw

Chapter 6: Dr. Mac
(The value of trust)
Suggested Reading: *Shame Off You* by Alan Wright
Suggested Listening: "I Will Be Here for You" by Michael W. Smith http://www.youtube.com/watch?v=bruLafuiu80

THE FEAR
Chapter 7: Timothy
(The paralyzing power of fear—An overview)
Suggested Reading: The Twelfth Angel by Og Mandino
Suggested Listening: "Rise Up" by R. Kelly http://www.youtube.com/
watch?v=vrYs0iYuEVc&feature=player_embedded

Chapter 8: Travis
(The fear of failure)
Suggested Viewing: Denzel Washington's Commencement Address to
the University of Pennsylvania (2011) http://www.youtube.com/
watch?v=vpW2sGlCtaE
Suggested Reading: *The Bunt* by Don Blackwell
Suggested Listening: "Dare You to Move" by Switchfoot
http://www.youtube.com/watch?v=iOTcr9wKC-o&feature=youtu.be

Chapter 9: Junnuh
*(The fear that a healthier, happier you is a distant and
irretrievable memory)*
Suggested Viewing: *The Legend of Baggar Vance* (2000) and
("The Woods") http://www.youtube.com/watch?v=_Mk2Tca88Xo
Suggested Listening: "One Clear Voice" by Peter Cetera
http://www.youtube.com/watch?v=MNXKkJeBXFI

Chapter 10: Brock
(The fear that we can't, before we've even tried)
Suggested Viewing: http://www.youtube.com/watch?v=XyPkUXGq1S0
and *Facing the Giants* (2006)
Suggested Reading: *The Little Engine that Could* by Watty Piper
Suggested Listening: "The Voice of Truth"—Casting Crowns
http://www.youtube.com/watch?v=KwsvqVmFV6Y

Chapter 11: Courtney
(The power of our gifts and the corresponding fears of success and of disappointing others)
Suggested Reading: *A Return to Love: Reflections on the Principles of A Course in Miracles* by Marianne Williamson
Suggested Viewing: Coach Carter (2005)
Suggested Listening: "I Hope You Dance" by Lee Ann Womack

Chapter 12: The First Step
(The fear of venturing out)
Suggested Reading: *Oh, the Places You'll Go!* by Dr. Seuss
Suggested Listening: "Walk on Water" by Britt Nicole
http://www.youtube.com/watch?v=Et00UNFDjVM

THE HEALING
Chapter 13: Mr. Fix-It
(Losing the control we never really had)
Suggested Listening: "When You Say Nothing At All" by Allisun Krauss
http://www.youtube.com/watch?v=_bNfay6HiUo&feature=related

Chapter 14: The Girl on the Park Bench
(The freedom that comes from realizing that we may not have all the answers)
Suggested Listening: "I Believe" by Nikki Yanofsky
http://www.youtube.com/watch?v=7v0o27BPIIk

Chapter 15: The Miners
(Contrary to popular belief, hope is not a light that awaits our arrival at the end of the proverbial tunnel)
Suggested Viewing: Scene from *The Shawshank Redemption*
http://www.youtube.com/watch?v=hWUfFwoe8ko

Suggested Listening: "The Storm is Over Now" by R. Kelly
http://www.youtube.com/watch?v=6Cg_A-zCkIE

Chapter 16: The Monarch
("Just when the caterpillar thought its life was over"—A case study in patience)
Suggested Reading: *Hope for the Flowers* by Trina Paulus
Suggested Listening: "Patience" by Take That
http://www.youtube.com/watch?v=273eSvOwpKk&ob=av2e

Chapter 17: A Young Mother and Her Two Little Boys
(And other everyday acts of courage)
Suggested Reading: *The Courage Code* by Megan Raphael and Jennifer Byron and *Facing the Lion, Being the Lion* by Mark Nepo
Suggested Listening: "Courage Is" by The Strange Familiar0
http://www.youtube.com/watch?v=cXrWRM0E6YA&feature=related

Chapter 18: Derek and Jim
(Finding joy and wonder in the uncertainty of the journey)
Suggested Viewing: http://www.youtube.com/watch?v=HFKpZnok10s
Suggested Listening: "The Climb" by Miley Cyrus http://www.youtube.com/watch?v=NG2zyeVRcbs and
"The Dance" by Garth Brooks http://www.youtube.com/watch?v=_kzLlgg5ZxM

Chapter 19: The Gorilla
(Embracing the sometimes jagged, often ill-fitting pieces of the puzzles of our lives)
Suggested Listening: "Unwritten" by Natasha Bedingfield http://www.youtube.com/watch?v=hdQRyYXorHQ

Chapter 20: Chuck

(Giving is living)

Suggested Viewing: Craig Thompson's Commencement Address at the University of Maryland (2010) http://www.youtube.com/watch?v=0Wn_bpgDARc

Suggested Reading: *The Giving Tree* by Shel Silverstein

Suggested Listening: "With My Own Two Hands" Jack Johnson and Ben Harper

http://www.youtube.com/watch?v=i7q98vL1Xy0

Chapter 21: TPD

(Taking a closer look at "The Total Package Dad")

Suggested Listening: "Firework" by Katy Perry http://www.youtube.com/watch?v=QGJuMBdaqIw&ob=av2e

and "Flawz" by Caitlin Crosby http://www.youtube.com/watch?v=R_PpRpYME10

CPSIA information can be obtained at www.ICGtesting.com
Printed in the USA
LVOW081958260613

340289LV00003B/4/P

9 781614 483298